# Poetically
## Pursued

*Love Came After Me*

# Erinn Imari

## Dedication

*For Amariah and Eden, you are my why, Mommie loves you*
*For Calvin, your voice pushed this to manifest, I'm thankful*
*For Valeria, your strength still amazes me*
*For J. Michele, because of you I've learned how to dance in the rain...I did it ma, I miss you*

## INTRODUCTION

Sometime before 6$^{th}$ or 7$^{th}$ grade, I was introduced to poetry. I don't even remember how we met. I didn't even know her name. I don't recall if I read a book or heard someone recite it or where it came from. Between my mom and this English teacher who was a pioneer in nurturing my love for words, I fell for poetry like orange leaves as they caress the grass tips on Autumn's eve— easy love. She would challenge me to put words together that I wouldn't have otherwise even imagined...trains of thoughts I had never followed before. This newfound ability would serve as a very powerful coping tool in the years to come. So, do not laugh at the early writings I will share with you here. Poetry and I have grown much since those first recordings, but I want to be transparent and tell you where I started. I did not appear like someone who carried the internal battles that I'll describe along this journey. I was studious, mostly mannerable, funny, and responsible...most times, lol. If I didn't tell you, you wouldn't know to suspect a thing!

I was introduced to my Savior by Valeria Bell. She was truly a praying mother—she definitely took us to church. On Sunday, Tuesday, Wednesday, Saturday-LOL! I know now that her prayers reached heaven for me then, often. Don't get it twisted...I didn't realize how heavy this was while I was going through it. This book has the beauty of hindsight. I can articulate and understand now what I didn't know then. I didn't have the language then. The beauty of this process is being able to carry the proper language and emotional intelligence back to the little girl in me and healing her from the inside out. So often, voices aren't heard, cries are ignored, and tragedy could have been prevented if they were. I hope my story encourages those that need to speak and those that need to hear as well as be heard. Writing poetry did not come from any deep inspiration for me. It came more as an escape, if just for a moment, from my life's reality. I wasn't interested in a correct format or a proper structure. I simply enjoyed expressing my inner voice, somehow, someway. Poetry gave a voice to words I was afraid to speak, to emotions I didn't want to feel or know how to feel, and thoughts I didn't know I had. Poetry became my confidant, my soul mate. Whenever I needed them, pen and paper were within reach; for so long, poetry was my only coping mechanism.

Along the way, God used my poetry to open my eyes and ears to a whole new idea and level of understanding. Using this gift, He spoke to me and through me. While healing me, He showed me it was okay to express how I felt. Poetry was a healthy way to convey those feelings. My thoughts, emotions, and words during these times, understood exactly who I was and accepted me; unpolished, unfinished, and raw. Poetry loves me! This is my story to share. My smiles, frowns, and hurts were the necessary parts of my healing and restoration. During this process, I knew God was speaking to me and I responded. I will share what entering God's marvelous light was like for me and why I chose to stay. I hope my poetic voice will ring in your hearts as you walk through my journey and witness my life's transformation. Now before we embark, you should know that this is a collection of my initial work. Be gentle with my beginnings and my perceptions of actual happenings. It is my truth. I was led and wanted to share it. Oh! I forgot to mention, I like intimate walks. I was hoping you'd enjoy taking a stroll with me—beside the quiet streams of my memories, invading the dark forests of my past traumas as we hold hands and dive into the vast corridors of my deepest, remembered places—some were great, and others…well let's explore, shall we?!

## VOLUME 1

Just before my freshman year in high school, I had become very "rebellious," as I had heard it described by others. A lot had led to and played a part in these "rebellious" events, but my reaction to what was happening in my life had just begun to unfold. Early on in my childhood, there were aversive memories that left lasting sour tastes on the palate of my mind, yet because it wasn't the culture nor was it encouraged to share feelings or emotions, I buried these memories without even being aware that I had done so. Watch out Pontiac, Michigan! Eastside, Lookout Dr. was the place to be, honey. This was where it was at! Everybody on the street knew our family. How that small, blue, 3-bedroom, 9-window, 1-bathroom, boxed kitchen house held 9 and many times more people at once is beyond me. There were us 7 and then our cousins would come to stay too, for extended lengths of time. I had a front row seat to all the action! I am the youngest, most brilliant, liveliest, and shiniest of 7 children. What?! You know I had to hype it up!! LOL. Needless to say, there were many comparisons and a lot to live up to. Being criticized, picked on, challenged, and made fun of often was part of the culture. It made us tough, but it also wounded. You didn't know to question what was considered normal. Hear me out though because as dysfunctional as many of our upbringings were…kids these days, ha, yeah—I'll stop right there. This is about upward movement (giggles at the thought of my children surviving Lookout Dr. days.) So…telling jokes and roasting each other was what you did.

I hated it. Partly because I sucked at it, but also because it didn't feel good talking about people like that all the time. Like, geesh, say something nice why don't cha. Something in me early on knew that I didn't want the culture's norm to be my norm…it was not ok just because it was "ok." Blame it on the Cosby Show, but I didn't want to accept it, just because. I wanted better—you know, something different. I wanted the mushy, emotional stuff! I wanted hugs, kisses, secret handshakes, words of encouragement, pats on the back after a good talking to cause you knew you had messed up..,you know—LOVE!

With a combination of my TV family fantasies and my real-life realities, it's safe to say that for a while, my ideas and definitions of identity and self-worth were a bit contorted and marred. Now, in earshot, this doesn't seem that bad, and all of it wasn't. I'm sure, at heart, it wasn't the intent of the culture to harm, dismantle, and strip away each other's sense of worth and confidence. A thing becomes normal because it becomes routine and keeps us sane inside of so much insanity. Routine is born from comfort, and dare I say even from survival. 'This is how I've been doing it, so why does it need to change?' Sometimes, what helped us survive will not sustain us even though it helped to prepare us for the next part of the journey. Change is always necessary for growth. Today, I understand that much more clearly. Then, my psyche did not always receive it in the way it was being served. I didn't know the jokes were just for laughs. Heck, those who were really good at it could totally throw some stingers.

"Daaaaannnnnggggg, he roasted you, dawg!!!" as the crowd would say to add in on the effects. Vividly, I recall my brother using my 3-foot doll to demonstrate how he did some guy after a basketball game. My poor doll never stood a chance. The aftermath was broken limbs, cocked eyes, and bald patches in what used to be her black girl magic hair. I had to be like 6 or 7. I was devastated. I called my mom at work to inform her of the death. "Mommy, do something. He broke her into pieces!" I exclaimed. Growing pains of life, right? These people would just about have me convinced that I was adopted. I can laugh now, but then?! I didn't know that my siblings making fun of my dad's addiction was a jovial or light matter. For me, it was heavy every time; it was real hurt. I wanted to fight every time…and would, even as the tears strolled down my cheekbones. I couldn't interpret my mother's intent while I was being called every name that wasn't mine, as her simply and only wanting the best for me. It felt personal, like, uh, does she like me?! Since becoming a parent myself, I know now—but then!! I didn't possess the fundamental or mental development necessary to see the harsh delivery and the brash lectures quite that way. My mom was strong because she had to be. And until I knew her story, all I saw was a mean mama. That perception of my mom grew into the belief that she didn't like me, which developed into, I don't think she loves me. This ate away at my identity, confidence, and how or if I even valued myself. I thought, "at least, if she does love me, I don't know it."

My siblings often called me weird. Many times, I became the butt of the joke—Denise Huxtable of my family. How rude (Full House)!! Sometimes, I would laugh too! Delivery is EVERYTHING!!...but still pretending! I guess it's fair to say I missed the big picture, a lot! As I would try to do my roasts, I took my time to think about the success I'd have coming after once I hit my punch line. My punches never quite connected. "You octopus explosion head! You ole jellyfish on crack! You so ugly your face is running away!" Yeah! I could never get the funny part of the joke to work in my favor. Plain and simple, I was horrible at comedy, roasting, riddles—you name it. I mean, that's who I was then, so green! I didn't always see the things right in front of me, a child's understanding for sure. I caught on sometimes to some things...but most things, I questioned. The naturally cleverness for them didn't always stand out for me. I was very naïve back then, and it cost me a lot later on down the line. What else did I know? How could I know? Who was there to warn me these things would go on to create 'am I enough' insecurities and self-conscious, identity confusion in the years to come? No one knows beforehand when things will or won't or even what things in life will cause the greatest wounds. I had no idea how ugly things would get before they were no longer ugly. I was living life as best I knew how. Being a kid, imitating, repeating, taking it all in—and still, I was visited by feelings of worthlessness...not ever being accepted. My siblings were amazing people to live up to. They were big, strong, confident, and fearless—from my point of view, they had it all worked out. "Show me," I thought. Where was my strength? I learned to mask it very well behind hard work, determination, and good grades...you know—the *normal* stuff. I hid it so well that I would sometimes forget myself...until. It always comes back, doesn't it?! The thing is, these thoughts and feelings I'm sharing are not abnormal at all. People just didn't talk like this back then, so Erinn, with all her emotions, was laughed at and disregarded...in those regards! I had this burning inside— a desire—a picture that pulled me and centered me at times, and it was bigger than I could articulate to myself at the time, or anyone for that matter. In hindsight, I know something was guiding me...bigger than me, ya know?! Can we say but God!!!

I'd actually become aware of the anger and animosity that was building inside me around age 13. By then, I could identify that it existed. I had seen many nights that were full of screams, loud noises, fights, slamming doors, or broken glass to match the promises. I can hear the cursing and the banging still in my ear. There were nights when the thunderstorms weren't even scary anymore. The roaring from inside was enough to make the rain hush. I recall this one night in particular, when I was 9 years old, which was so different from the others. This time, I had come out of my room to stop the fighting. It was cold. Not like we didn't have working heat, but cold, and I couldn't comprehend why. I saw my mom trying to go for the door, but my dad was standing in front of her saying, "Val, stop!", but mom wasn't yelling anymore. Instead, I witnessed a quiet surrender as she slid, in slow motion, to the floor in what seemed like defeat at first glance, but whatever it was, it was much deeper than I knew. I cannot tell you, but I remember being able to recognize there was something off; something was very wrong. This was not the norm. They would fight many times before, and nothing would change. My dad was an addict of alcohol and drugs. His lifestyle had been a tumultuous rollercoaster, gradually tearing the family up, yet at that age, in my eyes, he was just Daddy. I didn't see the bad choices or the weight they carried quite the same way my older siblings and mother did. They had seen a plethora of nights much worse than I'd witnessed. That quiet surrender would change everything! Life as I knew it was about to shape-shift drastically, and I nor it would ever be the same.

Here we are with this anger—this rage inside me all the time now. Why? It wasn't because of his bad habits, but because of the pounds and pounds of confusion and the whisper of its uncertainty—accompanied by a cycle of changes that were about to take place in my life without warning. See, Daddy was going to yet another rehab program, and this time it was out of state. I wanted my dad to get clean and sober. I really did, but I didn't want him to leave *me*. Dad and I were very close—at least to me (hahaha). No one else in this family saw me or allowed me to be ok in my "weird" like he did. Why did he have to go away? Why was he doing this to his family, to me, to us? He betrayed me and no one stopped him, no one cared to. Bill would never have done this to Claire. They would talk it out and then laugh and hug as the music cued in; then the screen would go to another scene because that next part was not for TV viewing (back in those days). The next day they would be fine. No grudge, no lingering unforgiveness…only love. Why is this not working in my house? Does no one hear me screaming? These changes taking place in my life, which I didn't believe were beneficial to Erinn, greatly impacted the direction my mental processing and perspectives would travel. This was ruining my fantasy, my only happy place. Daddy, you see, listened to me when I talked—you know, like actually shared how I was feeling about things—he didn't just hear my voice. I felt like he knew my soul and understood me for who I was underneath it all. He's the first one I revealed my poetry to—I was so unaware that he might have been high as a kite on something every time he listened; that didn't matter. I didn't know to care. My perspective is what was real to me, and somebody, Daddy, was listening. In those moments, I mattered. I had an ear, his ear, not a pencil and some paper. It was a real person who brought me the only sense of being authentically me as it related to other human beings. I never felt like I could really show it, all of me, that is. I don't even think this man was aware of my attachment to him. These moments were true and magical to me. I believed what I had to say mattered when talking to him. I mattered—and I desperately needed that validation and connection.

Those 3 months seemed like an eternity. That house just seemed so empty, and I was lonely. I wrote letters to God, a lot!

Just trying to express how I felt. As I think about it now, the fact that I felt like I had to sneak to write letters to God is preposterous…but—then I walked into my daughter's room one day and saw her jump. I said, "hey baby, what are ya doin?!" "Nothing, mommy," she'd say, "just writing in my journal." "OK!," I said as I left her in her privacy. It would dawn on me—I love it when God takes your mind back to understand a thing from a different angle. I remember being that child just like my daughter now, and I think the reason we were sneaking is because we had some things to share with God, and we didn't want Mommy or other family to feel like we were betraying or talking bad about them…but we were. We were telling it all to God. Spilling all the beans honey—"God, she did this, and did you know they said this to me, and…," oh yeah, we were writing it all. Thank God for prayer!! LOL! I can tell Him about it all, and I don't have to sneak (giggle).

I'd wait for my dad's phone calls like they were my air to breathe. I remember being able to sleep with my mom while he was gone…you know, with permission this time. Cause baby, I was in there anyway! Some moments were so perfect I never wanted them to end. We'd lay there watching *In the Heat of the Night or Murder She Wrote,* and she'd let me lay my head in her lap. Those moments were priceless jewels that are forever mine. Crazy thing is I know I have many great memories from childhood—with my mom and dad, aunts and uncles, with my siblings, my cousins, church family, and with friends too. That's the thing about trauma though. You don't always choose what you forget—or what you remember. Healing helps push the clouds away so at some point, you can see the great memories as they were and not overshadowed or darkened by the hurt they were coupled with. When I get together with my siblings today—boy, oh boy, let me tell you, the roar of laughter is humungous. There are still some scars there, but the love is real. Eventually, Dad returned from rehab. He was a changed man, alright. One might say that was great, and it was—I guess, but it didn't seem so great to me. I didn't know him anymore; *"Harpo, who dis man?"* I'd sit back and just watch him; he seemed so strange and foreign. Our talks weren't the same, and he seemed more like a stranger I wanted to know rather than a friend I had already known. As he was transitioning back into our lives, he and my mom were rekindling their long-lost flame, and he was acting like a *parent*. He started giving me rules and telling me what I could and couldn't do. I was definitely not accustomed to this coming from Daddy. It was always, "go ask your mom." Now this! Still, I stayed close; after all, he was still Daddy. Everyone thought I just behaved so badly, and I didn't want to listen. A "spoiled brat" was the label; she's got it too good. *It wasn't that*! No one noticed how dad's great new life was affecting *my* life. Nothing was ever explained to me, and it obviously wasn't registering accurately on its own. I mean, I don't know if I would have understood it all at the time, but hey, I would have liked the chance, I think. Kids don't usually just act out. Something caused it! I was confused, hurt, and furious. Who was *this* man, and where and what had he done with Daddy? MY DADDY!!! I had thoughts going through my mind that made me believe my mom was with another man, as if he wasn't my real dad. It really felt like she was cheating or something. Y'all, I'm serious! It felt gross to see them like that— all lovey dovey...almost unnatural—and it was *for me!* I'd NEVER seen it. I was getting some version of the Cosby Show, but uh—I saw it going differently in my mind as Will Smith's character from Hitch reported. Who knows how long it had been since they had been so close—and I surely wasn't adapting well to seeing it unravel. For many years, I tried to cover up what was happening on the inside. I didn't share the crazy thoughts that rummaged through my insides. I was always looking for something to make sense of it all, something to help me feel normal or accepted. I didn't share the increasing urge to do this and the curiosity to try that. I kept it to myself, pen and paper. I tried hard to be *regular* in my family's eyes, but it was only a matter of time before my insides bubbled out onto everybody's nicely paved streets for all to see. My cries had been silent for so long; I felt very alone, detached, and misunderstood. A diary shouldn't be the only voice of reason a child hears...puberty and major life changes, with no instruction or guidance, do not go hand in hand! Read that again! Teen years are harder than folks give it credit.

My coping skills must not have been up to par because I wasn't handling this the way I was expected to—taught to—raised to. Dad started going to church, and while he was gaining security, mine was being stripped from under me. I had an understanding of who God is, yet my faith wasn't strong enough (at the time) for this battle. I slowly drifted into the enemy's trap. And so, as it goes in every story…the illusion came. There was this guy who I thought was a *forever* kind of love. I would have given him the world if it were mine to hand out. *Sing Luther Vandross!!!* He was my new security, my knight in shining armor—*my normal*. He was a perfect illusion of what love looked like to me. So, I poured. Everything! All I had to give…was his.

## I AM WHO I AM

*My heart beats a tune. Sometimes, it even sings.*

*I often ask...is it speaking to my soul or speaking to me?*

*I have hidden emotions and unlearned knowledge of my own self.*

*Who am I?*

*I am a woman! Yes, tall and slim, with a sunny, bright smile.*

*I am a daughter, a sister, an aunt, and a friend.*

*But do I really know who I am?*

*I'm seeking to find my inner self, devoting time to my mind.*

*To knowing and understanding my thoughts—to say what I feel and feel what I say.*

*But what am I saying?*

*There are waterfalls of love saturating my soul daily—flushing out all the impurities.*

*I am clean, I am free, and yes, I am a woman!*

*From my mother's bosom, to the suction of her warm breast.*

*As a child, I held her hand, and now I wave goodbye.*

*I often drift into a world where everything makes sense.*

*But when I come back, I find that still—I know nothing.*

*Naturally, poetic vibes emanate from the meditations of my organ of life,*

*My heart, that is...I write because it's who I am.*

*I am poetry, and it is I.*

*But again, I ask, who am I ?*

*I represent a seed that has begun to grow—I've been sown in fertile ground.*

*And I will sprout...my leaves are full of life, and my roots are too*
*deep to be dug out.*
*Though still a child, yet now, a child of God!*

*Who am I?*

*I am the rib that was broken to create such a delicate vessel!*

## A CHILD

*I truly think no one cares! Yet no one knows I feel this way because I've learned how to wear a mask. I know how to put up a façade and look the way everybody expects and already perceives how I should look. I've learned to hide my pain and the embers of agony. I hide it with smiles and with laughter, with silliness and busy activities.*

*Yet inside, oh but inside—I'm so lonely...in this all by myself.*

**I'm too ugly for anybody to really like me; I can't run and play anymore because I'm too fat. I stink because Momma can't afford to wash my clothes. They have holes in them anyway, so why bother? I just don't fit in. I'm always being excluded, last to be picked for anything.**

*I feel like the people that are in my life are only there because of obligation, not because they really wanna be. I don't wanna talk about it though, because I don't wanna bother Momma with my little problems. It's just that I feel so empty and meaningless. People think it's no big deal, but I don't think I'm gonna make it through this.*

**Momma always says I'm gonna be just like Daddy— whom I've never seen 'cause Papa's a rolling stone. Or she says I'll be like my sister who's at the corner of every stop sign waving her goods like she's selling cookies and freshly squeezed lemonade.**

*I find everything, except good and positive things, to get into; I think it's because I have no direction. No one loves me enough to correct me or guide me in the right way. I told you so; no one cares! They may not actually say that, but every action speaks it loud and clear.*

**Momma's boyfriend always puts his arm around me, yet only when Momma's not looking. He rubs on my legs with a crooked grin on his face, and I just close my eyes—trying to take myself to a better place.**

*When my sister babysits me, she makes weird noises in the bedroom, and someone is in there with her. She just makes me stay in the living room and watch TV until she comes out. And she looks so tired when she comes out!*

**I always see my brother pushing his girlfriend around, and he tells me to take notes. He says men own women and that they will learn to obey one way or another. He says it's the man's job to teach them their duties and how to keep their mouth shut. He says a real man hustles and knows that money is everything—said I better get rich...or at least die trying.**

*A child—a gift to be cherished and nurtured, not a task to be neglected.*

*A child—everything you tell them they are, everything you tell them they aren't,*

*A blessing in every aspect!*

*A child—a seed that if watered and nourished, will grow and blossom into a perfect miracle to behold.*

*A child—a dream that needs a vision and a leader to follow.*

> *You are a child of God—fearfully and wonderfully made.*
>
> *His fingerprints are all over you.*
>
> *So the next time someone tells you, you can't...*
>
> *You look at them, smiling, and say—I AM is my Father;*
>
> *Therefore, I can!*

## COLORS OF VISION

*Feelings and emotions I can't describe; heaviness has kissed my eyes—wide open.*

*Wondering how He could allow—my Master, my Creator, why is He sitting back now?*

*Don't you know my cry, don't you feel my agony?*

*Not allowed to give up, not allowed to walk astray, no room to give in.*

*No, my attempts to indulge are forever spotlighted, so I cannot budge.*

*A scream, perhaps, so my hurt can be acknowledged.*

*Or maybe a stunt of some sort—what can I do—or say?*

*It's no longer a dull ache or a lingering sting; it's more like the memories want to cling.*

*Choking my impulses, ripping away the stillness of repression,*

*Pounding into my mental channels, what if, how could, and why me?*

*I've escaped enough to say…I'm ok.*

*Desperately crawling into sanity and reaching for normalcy.*

*No matter how far away I get, the heaviness has kissed my eyes—wide open.*

*And I can never run from the framed art hanging on my internal walls—*

*Blue walls of inspiration, red vows meant for trust, faded, yellow affections and white intimacies with black delicacies…green mountains of new desire, while Heaven poured orange drops of fire and passion.*

*Deep valleys and high hills—no way to shield the sun, or its rays. Just a phase?*

*Palms turned up, sweat falling on each side, heart races, my pulse confides—within the mere thought, my stomach turning inside...*

*WHY DO YOU SEEK MY SOUL?*

*HAVE YOU NOT ALREADY TAKEN IT ALL?*

*No, you didn't—you left a flicker down low—still burning, still growing!*

*I am yet alive, though still, heaviness has kissed my eyes—wide open!*

## LOST MEMORIES

*It seems as though I've lost my soul within.*

*The shining star that once shone has gone from me.*

*I feel so empty inside because my love went away.*

*Tell me, when...*

*And tell me, why love couldn't stay?*

*The depths of my love could not be measured.*

*Every time I felt love's touch, it grew more.*

*The walls of my heart are descending rapidly.*

*The smile...*

*My strength every day,*

*I swear, without love...*

*My tears will drown me.*

*You left me.*

*The pain—it's burning,*

*It's burning, like an inferno.*

*I just thought you should know.*

## MY DADDY, WHEN NO ONE ELSE WOULD

*Daddy, you're a step above the rest!*

*Always up for a new test,*

*Constantly pushin' away the shadows of doubt,*

*To understand what this thing called life is all about.*

*When no one else would—I can't possibly repay, but I wish I could.*

*Full expressions cannot be made.*

*For Daddy, my heart, you won, and I learned how to trust.*

*So just to tell you how I feel was certainly a must.*

*When no one else would—I can't possibly repay, but I wish I could.*

*When no one else would, you understood my cry.*

*When no one else tried, my shedding tears, you'd dry.*

*When no one else would—I can't possibly repay, but I wish I could.*

*All I have to give is the undying love of a daughter.*

*And please, do believe…I remember everything you taught her.*

*When no one else would—I can't possibly repay, but I wish I could.*

*A meek, strong man of God—built with sincerity and full of heart.*

*You've been my best man from the start—and we'll always be two peas in a pod.*

*When no one else would—I can't possibly repay, but I wish I could.*

## PAPER AND BALLPOINT PENS

*Silent cries, tryin' to hide. Lonely nights, whispering hopes in the morning's new light.*

*But I'm much too full of hurt.*

*Burning pain inside my soul—I'm so cold.*

*My desire is slowly fading. I pretend everything's alright, yet I've been crying far too long.*

*There's someone here inside wanting to be reborn, revived.*

*I listen to the melodies of my heart, but the sound is so construed— I can no longer tell them apart...my voice is too faint! I'm in desperate need of a clean slate.*

*I'm in this betwixt, and all alone, cause no one knows how to fix what it is I'm feeling.*

*People pretend to care; however, my tears are my load to bear— life is truly unfair.*

*My agenda or their agenda?*

*I'm sick of doing things to prove to this person or that person that I'm more than the label they give me.*

*I find more comfort in quiet winds and moonlit skies than I do in human ties.*

*So if I fall, who will catch me? If I cry, who will hear?*

*Because sharing how I feel is my biggest fear.*

*It's foreign and unlearned.*

*So I continue with the pouring of my tear-filled eyes to endless lakes and blind dates...*

*My peace is at stake.*

*Whom is there to hear my lonely nights and silent cries?*

*My companions, my friends, my soul mates…paper and ballpoint pens!*

## DETERMINING THOUGHTS

*I sometimes think of life and what it's all about.*

*My mind begins to search for what I'm being taught.*

*The trials we must face,*

*Along with strength from God—we'll have grace.*

*Am I walking the righteous path, or am I taking for granted what*

*I have?*

*Salvation He freely gave!*

*So gratefully, will I go to my grave.*

*Striving to make faith my daily song.*

*God is of love and truth—I am living proof!*

*Who holds my soul?*

*The one of whom I just told!*

## THE IMAGE

*I'm looking at me—in the future—I see the way I want to be.*

*It's all a beautiful, vivacious image fluttering through my mind.*

*As I gaze at this vision—it's a window of endless possibilities.*

*Yet, I am overcome by repeated fears. I know that fear should not be here.*

*So I tell myself...No! I place my ear against these thoughts, and I listen for the answers.*

*The answers to all my foolish questions—In-A-Me—that's my worst enemy!*

*Erinn, why can't you just sit back and let God do His thang? Why won't you just,*

*Shut up?—sometimes, I get so caught up in all the "but's," the "it could's," and all those "what if's" that I miss out on God. His presence is the gift of life—the gift that gives without strife. A gift only from above—and as His Spirit invades my thoughts and begins to speak, exposing where I'm weak—to my open heart, He speaks...*

*The only person you are hindering when you choose to abide in dead thoughts—is you!*

*Thoughts of "what if" are an unnecessary pain...dumping pounds of anxious rain that stain my believing and understanding.*

*As I open my eyes, I become one with this new image of myself—I take hold of the truth—the realization that supernaturally reminds me of the revelation that uh...together, somehow, it will all work out for me. I love God—He called me with purpose!*

*I know this because He was sacrificed, that I would be excluded*
*from the penalty.*
*Of a life lived in fire's eternity.*
*Covered in red, the blood—redeemed, He bled—for me!*
*Created in His image—His child—I'm His—image and all.*

## ENTANGLED FROM WITHIN

*My eyes burn from the tears that never fell; my soul gasps for the air that drifted away.*

*The pain inside is deeper than my words can travel.*

*It's in my blood stream and has interrupted my demeanor.*

*My body aches with depression.*

*I don't recognize my own face anymore. I try to ignore, but the numbness has gone for sure.*

*Where do I begin to mend? Where is there a shoulder to lean? On whom can I depend?*

*The agony of knowing the Word, yet so far from instruction; having been filled, yet no power to stand upon. I tried crying out, but no words form in my mouth.*

*The thoughts are trapped in my mind because insanity has encircled my will. I take a step, only to stumble from fear of failure…so I just keep still.*

*My spirit moans within, wanting to taste of His goodness.*

*I imagine myself in my Father's arms, being rocked, and sailing away from the storm.*

*The pressure I can no longer contain—my strength is gone; I'm left all alone with no one to call my own.*

*I tried my mother, but not even her touch can heal my brokenness.*

*I called Dad and his understanding was limited.*

*Sisters and brothers cannot tell me the issues of my heart.*

*I've lost sight of who I am, and fear has gripped me—stolen my light and I now sit in the coldness of the dark. Will this ever come to an end? Will my praise reach the Master's ear ever again? My vision is blurred, my soul is scarred, and my faith needs to be stirred—better yet, consoled.*

## ONE VOICE

*I know the source from whence I come, yet sometimes, I forget*
*Just how far He's brought me from.*
*A sound I often think I hear—making my eyes tear.*
*He's given so much, I've neglected a bunch—yet still, He loves me*
*so much!*
*I want to lie by His side as the sky grows high.*
*This wonder of life truly makes me sigh.*
*In awe of Adonai!*
*Where did such a love come about?*
*The battle that He fought—the infancy of a human mind could*
*never find.*
*It would take a millennium to figure it out.*
*But why should I pout?*
*I have life—the greatest gift of His love.*

## REALITY BURNING

*Have I really opened my eyes, or have I just blinked?*

*Sometimes, things just aren't as they appear.*

*Sometimes, life feels like an impossible knot. The more I struggle with it, the more tangled it gets.*

*Is there a way to get the knot out? Sure, there's always a solution to a problem, right?*

*Call for help...that doesn't work because no one hears me call. Try explaining the situation...no one understands.*

*Will there ever be anyone to hear me?? Who knows?*

*They say, don't give up; keep crying for help. But it never comes... What do I do then? I'm all twisted up in knots with no way to get free.*

*Are my knots too tight to get loose? Is there anyone who can help me be free?*

*Sometimes, I think I'll never know.*

*Running doesn't help either. The problems only follow. It's almost like they'll never go.*

*Leave the past behind me? Can I? That's a real challenge!*

*My name, Erinn, peace is what it means; but I never have peace.*

*Do you feel my pain? Do you hear my cry? Do you understand? Do you have an answer?*

*So they're my parents—does that mean they are never wrong? Who's to say?*

*Not me, of course.*

*Listen, do you hear me at all? Obviously not! What went wrong? Was it my childhood?*

*I didn't think it was 'that bad,' was it? I can't turn back the hands of time, even if it was*

*I can't erase the tears. Will my heart ever heal?*

*I want to do right. What's holding me back?*

*Pain, sorrow, heartache, and love's imitation are holding me back. I can't talk because I don't know how. How do you voice what even you don't understand? Besides, no one wants to listen to me and my struggles. No one understands me anyhow. Love...what is love? I know it exists; I know it's there. It just doesn't seem to care. Is Love hiding from me?*

*That's not it—it was there at some point. I think I lost contact. Maybe the number got changed.*

*One day, isn't that what they say? One day.*

# VOLUME 2

The more I wrote, the more it hurt. It was like a war was taking place inside me—*for* me. The words that came from within seemed to find their home so easily upon my notebook. When reading my own poems, my private thoughts on paper, the atmosphere was consoling in its own way. It was as if someone had put on paper, my very heart. In essence, I guess that was exactly what I'd done, huh? I didn't know how to share these emotions outside of my mind—at least not verbally—and one too many times, my behavior displayed the opposite of how I truly felt inside. Many nights, I cried from the emotional pain—desiring to 'feel' loved, fighting the aches of loneliness—wanting to belong to something, someone. I wanted so badly to crawl into my mother's arms and just lie there, yet anger, fear of rejection, and resentment stopped me every time. I couldn't let her see my vulnerabilities 'cause she'd think I was weak, and it would be another reminder that I wasn't good enough for her.

I was angry with her for not knowing how badly her little girl was hurting. I was angry that she didn't realize I was being bullied…and even though I didn't cower outwardly, I was a ball of fear inside. I was angry that I couldn't talk with her about the ganging up on me with verbal insults, massive intimidation, and literally walking behind me, spewing threats as I tried to walk away—constantly! I was angry because she didn't even notice. She didn't know that in 5th grade, I finally responded to the bullying and fought back with my fists. I blacked out and was still hitting the ground even after the principal had pulled the girl from beneath me. I was in such a raging panic that when they snapped me back into reality, I started screaming to the top of my lungs, "who else wants some?" I was angry at her for not protecting me from being exposed to things a child can't and shouldn't have to process alone. I was angry with her for not knowing how badly I wanted and needed to just be held by her and told, I love you. I was angry with her for inviting someone else into our life. This new man my dad had become was not welcomed, and *I* wanted that to be clear. I was angry with him for changing and abandoning our friendship, and I wanted things to make sense. THEY DIDN'T MAKE SENSE!!! I was so confused about how I felt. I needed my world to return to its origin. Even if the screaming, loud nights were wrong—so what it was dysfunctional, unhealthy, and toxic—it was my normal, and now that I didn't have it, I missed that *normal.*

Years passed by. I got older. I looked at this new truth every day, and it became routine to just inhale it and exhale it. I understood that this lifestyle was healthier for my dad than his previous one—I did.   That did not make it easier for me to adjust to and manage this complete shift in my home. Heart knowledge can take a while before reaching the brain, which sends a signal for us to now act according to what we know. You know... line your behavior up with what you believe and know to be true. Though I was dealing with many fearful thoughts, I knew I still had to face the fire and its heat. One side of me wondered, "God, are you still there? If so, please don't let go of me." While the other side said, "He already has." I knew what I had been taught. I knew God loved me, and would never leave me; He always helps in hard times. These just seemed like empty words to me. They weren't helping me to cope or deal any better with my situation. I didn't know how to apply their meaning to how I felt. I couldn't wait for God to help because I wanted Daddy back right then and there. "Dad," I'd think out loud, "don't you see your baby girl hurting?"

Then, there was my knight in shining armor. He wasn't such a knight after all, but I loved this guy so much I thought he was the air that supplied my lungs to breathe. He had his life to live, and I became a ready convenience rather than his *forever* love. I tried giving him more of me, yet instead of feeling accepted and special—I felt less and less meaningful to myself and to him. Hearing our story would make some believe we had a real thing going, especially the way *I* told the story. Yall know what's up!! (hahaha) Truth was, I felt most insecure when I was with him. I couldn't let him see the damaged girl I was for real. I had to pretend, so I did. I knew the kind of girls he was attracted to; I tried to become her. I failed repeatedly, over and over again. The real *me* would tell on me every time. Yesterday, he saw me get jumped for the 2$^{nd}$ time; today, he found a cigarette, and tomorrow, he sees me hanging out on the block cursing, being the tomboy I was, or just acting silly. I tried to be someone better for him, but all I really wanted was for him to love me for me, the real me—

the broken, silly, confused, wounded, care-free, empty, free-spirited, lost me! Just for him to choose *me!* I wasn't chosen, though. He was willing to keep having me around, so I was willing to keep up the façade. For me—it was genuine. One night, I went to his house. There was nothing special or different about this night. He would always sneak me in. He opened the back door, and we headed to the basement. I didn't notice the driveway was empty or that he opened the back door with comfort and not with a fear of being caught. I was high off simply knowing I was now with him. I fell deeper into the temporary reality of having him all to myself. In my mind, this was heaven. He had no idea of the vivid, live, in-color fantasy that motivated my every move. We talked and cuddled. He was gentle and sweet to the very end. I tell you, if this wasn't real for him, man, did he sure know how to make me believe it was? He was attentively into me!

Then—it happened…the moment in time that would shake the very foundation I thought we stood on. I don't remember what song was on the radio; I could no longer hear it. Had I put my bra back on? Had I ever taken it off? Was I under the cover because it got really hot—I don't know how our conversation slid this way or if I made a sound when the tears ran from my eyes, racing to the edge of my chin. What I do remember is him telling me all the women he'd been with besides me and how stupid I felt for loving him as much as I did. I remember my face being drenched from crying while I dressed and leaving so fast that I didn't notice the car in the driveway until I was a block away. I looked back and thought to myself, "damn, his mom was home!" As I thought out loud all the way to my sister's house, I strategized over and over how I could never allow him to hurt me like that again. It's unfortunate that I had to experience such a low, but it was a turning point I'll never forget and still remain thankful for.

For relief from these emotional mountains, I ran to different friends, anything fun, various drugs, anything fun, casual sex, anything fun, never-ending pours of alcohol, and anything that gave me the adrenaline rush that offered the escape I longed for. See, when my knight wasn't around, I was in complete control, or so I thought—from my point of view. My confidence had come in, my swag—I owned it. My name was known, and being bullied was far behind me. My squad and I—we called the shots, and dared anyone to step in the wrong direction. I learned quickly how to ease my dreadful reality and soften the blow of pain that constantly beat within. I got tough, callous, mean, big, strong, brave, and fearless—all the attributes I envisioned for a person who was in charge. It was late at night, after the rush was gone, that I would fall to my knees and whisper, *"Help me, I know You can, God, please."*

## FRUSTRATION

*I want to go OFF!*

*I want to allow my anger to express itself freely.*

*With no limitation, no obligation, just regulation and initiation.*

*My fist balls, my heart pounds, and my blood capillaries feel like they just might burst!*

*My insides are bubbling with volcanic lava heat, and the words are climbing up my throat and pushing against my lips too intensely to stop.*

*Lord, help!*

*My flesh is ALIVE—die, die, die!*

*Whew, I'm ok...I was just frustrated.*

## EMOTIONAL

*Sometimes, thinking of him hurts so much that I hold it all inside.*

*When I cry—there just aren't enough tears.*

*No matter the weight that tries to pull me down—love won't let me let go.*

*At times, I find myself in a daze, and there's no life in me except the throb within.*

*Someone quick—I can't breathe!*

*The thought of missing him is suffocating—detached but aware of what I've become,*

*Emotional.*

*All the pain, nonstop drowning in the pain—I'm numb.*

*I can't even feel the tub's hot water as I emerge my body.*

*Those arms that held me so tightly,*

*That touch, gently...invites me.*

*Where's that smile that calmed the wild flares?*

*Where is the one that soothes the darkness and cares?*

*Quiets my deepest fears,*

*It's not negotiable, I'm emotional.*

*Where is that one?*

## MIRRORS IN REVERSE

*You think you being strong is your strength—I say it's your greatest weakness.*

*Your alleged strength caused void, lack, and insecurity.*

*I contribute my inadequacies to all your proclaimed perfection.*

*You never let me see you cry—I never saw you hurt—are you even human?*

*Your criticisms of me were so diligent I thought I'd never make you proud.*

*Your comparisons made the margins impossible to reach.*

*A child, suffocated, by your acclaimed toughness,*

*Instead of tenderness and warmth.*

*I remember a glacial touch and a numbness to my pain.*

*In my most vulnerable moments, all I see is you walking the other way.*

*Now, I struggle to cry because I feel weak.*

*I can't ever get tired or want to rest because I was taught to keep going,*

*No matter the weight.*

*I'm afraid of my pain because it confuses my brain—*

*Am I?—Should I be hurting?*

*But why should my spirit be so vexed?*

*Jesus wept!—He felt, and he displayed it.*

*Sometimes, all it takes is a demonstration.*

## WORDS

*Don't really have any words that are attracted to this paper, just thoughts that require being released like vapor.*

*It seems like putting that exact feeling at this exact moment on paper is impossible,*

*yet still, I'll attempt.*

*It seems that I'm entrapped by the walls of my environment.*

*Strangled by the thoughts of others—words being unleashed that go unheard, yet intensively, potent.*

*They come back to whisper in my ear, and without a trail, have infected me with this dis ease.*

*As I ponder why these emotions have come upon me, I am inflamed with indecisive conclusions.*

*The air I am breathing offers no oxygen, and my lungs are filling with disgust.*

*This un-ease, what does it mean? The prefix 'dis' means the opposite of or the absence of, while ease is the state of being comfortable, freedom from pain or discomfort.*

*So, it seems that, in this state of disease, there is an absence of comfort. And why?*

*The music is not soothing, and the soft chatter of people talking in the background is louder than ever. But why?*

*The chair I rest in no longer offers support, for to my weight has been added twenty plus pounds of the rage that wants to burst through—through the receptors of anger and neural transmitters of the guilty stimuli that have stimulated this dis-ease.*

*And as this exact moment changes because of the extension of time from the last exact moment, I am overcome again by this feeling I can't quite name, can't quite describe. Once again, my thoughts have been invaded. This time, however, it's a smooth transition. I don't even remember the point behind these words, yet I do know this...I feel better!*

## MISSED LOVE

*When this first started, I really wasn't into you.*

*But after all that we've been through,*

*I just can't seem to let you go.*

*I never thought my love for you could grow this strong.*

*There are no limits to the things I'd do.*

*Tell me, please, what happened to my boo?*

*We've shared so many memories.*

*Enough to last a lifetime.*

*Where did I go wrong?*

*Tell me what I said, or what I did to make you walk away?*

*I tell myself that I've got to be crazy to keep running back to you.*

*All those other guys compared only to a breeze that flew away.*

*But no, you were that chill that went up my spine.*

*It just wouldn't leave me alone.*

### GOD IS

*God is...*

*My Motivation when I had no goals.*

*My Healer when I didn't know how sick I was.*

*My Peace in the midst of confusion.*

*God is...*

*My Comforter when I felt so all alone.*

*My Savior when I was lost.*

*My Father who wipes away every tear.*

*God is...*

*My Sight in all my dark tribulations.*

*My Friend who cares for me in my time of need.*

*My All in all!*

*God is...*

## COLLAGE

*My life feels like a map of the world that has been ripped apart until every country landed in the wrong place. However, in my real world, it's my emotions that have been shattered and scattered to the point that I wish I couldn't feel what it's like to feel. To the ears that listen, yet only curiously with wonder, not attentively or close enough to care, my cry for help sounds like pure worship, while my worship sounds like a cry for help. The tear from my eye looks like I've been touched by the Spirit, yet in true essence, my tear is a physical manifestation of my soul—a soul that is vexed, lonely, and confused. Lord, my life is your artwork. You created this world, please, put my countries back in order!*

## DID YOU KNOW

*Even though you didn't know the way your words opened my heart,*

*Like a footprint in the freshly fallen white snow.*

*My soul has been exposed to a new horizon.*

*At night, when the pensive rain is comfortably falling, that is when I think of you most.*

*Then the feeling in my body goes numb—as long as I live, of our love will I boast.*

*Well, did you know—definitive utterances allow the heart to breathe?*

*Only your verdant ways were the cause of your blindness—tears, but not of joy.*

*Came ever so slowly.*

*In your arms, I could hide forever because the sweet embrace chased all the pain away.*

*You and I always could be together as long as the wind sings to my heart.*

*The breath-taking flame in your eye intensely burns ever so bright.*

*It is the guiding light that covers my body with an uncontrolled tingle.*

*Loving you is the motivation of my heart's beat.*

*Slowly surpassing surprise, it always seems.*

*Through the winter skies is a beautiful sound of passionate warm music when you're around.*

*Emotion is the internal plea—why can't you just see?*

*How life is all about change and making the best without knowing what's going to happen next?*

*Dear God,*

*I am going through a very stressful time in my life right now. I know You know because I can still feel Your love holding on to my soul. Lord, I have no idea what is happening in my mind, but I do know that I need You so much right now. Lord, I feel like the devil is trying his best to take my soul. I need Your understanding, Your wisdom, and Your guidance. Lord, take me back to the place where I received Your Spirit. Lord, take me back to the place where I first believed. Jesus, I am laying all my burdens on You. I need a helping hand to show me how to let go and let God. You, above any, know my pain is real, and I know You would not put more on me than I could bear, yet Lord, I feel overwhelmed. Trials come and go, yes—but right now, I'm calling on the name of Jesus for my salvation. Lord, You said I am Your child. I rebuke the devil in the name of Jesus. He shall not have the victory over me. I am Your child, and that I will stay.*

*Lord, I pray this prayer in Your name—that I may be blessed with Your love—that You may show me that no weapon formed against me shall prosper. Show me, Jesus, that this battle is not mine, and I don't have to fight it.*

*In the name of Jesus,*

*Amen!*

## FOREVER ALWAYS

*I've always wanted you, and I love the things you do.*

*Like the soothing touch of your hand makes me want you as my man.*

*Being with you has only been my dream—sometimes, though, it seems so real.*

*Please let me know the deal 'cause I want you like whipped cream.*

*Your precious ways make me love you more—more each day.*

*And I think of you and me sitting on the dock of the bay.*

*As your gentle smell gives my heart wings to soar,*

*Could it be—you and me?*

*Could you hold me close all night, making my heart feel so right?*

*Forever and ever, I'll love you always; please, tell me, though.*

*Cause I'm beginning to exit from this fantasy phase until you let me know.*

*When will I get my chance to have this dance?*

*Can you kneel, speak, and tell me—how you really feel?*

### WHAT IS LOVE IF IT AIN'T REAL?

*I still think of him often. Closing my eyes as I remember his smell and the scent of his hair—feeling his hands move down my sides, appreciating the softness of his lips,*

*As I traced each dip with my fingertips.*

*My thoughts are bombarded daily. Reminiscing on how he made me feel like a lady, in a garden full of roses, only I mattered.*

*Supple wet kisses, soothing grips, as he clutched my body so firmly, every muscle that could, began to constrict.*

*The longing turned into throbbing, and the throbbing became extended nights...*

*Cuddled in each other's embrace, pretending like time had been erased—and I, I was wrapped inside these two brown figures that made me hotter with each touch.*

*I remember as these members held me, words drifted into my ear telling me I was safe.*

*This was my kingdom; he was my king, and I was his queen.*

*I began to ponder these thoughts, and before I could stop it, to the bottom of my face was a tear—for I had neglected to remember he was somebody else's man.*

*So you see, all the while, it was only lies being whispered into the ears of my soul.*

*Lies that had once again broken my courage to believe in love.*

*Now lift up your eyes and look at me, remember me—you see me every day and you never know it. I'm that strong, resilient, independent, and self-sufficient black woman.*

*"Just a vacancy. Love don't live here anymore. You abandoned me. Love don't live here anymore."*

*What do you do when you've lost sight of real love?*

*Sing Mary...I'm searching for a real love—have you seen him?*

## VOLUME 3

Hey junior year! Oh wait, I forgot. Here comes another shift. I was now in a private Christian school; it seemed to be having a positive impact. Due to back-to-back fights, my mom was fed up with the public school system. There was no resolution to any of the situations that kept my mother in the principal's office. The cause of the fights wasn't heard, but the solution to the fights was the same, leave school. No alternative measures were taken, no preventative assistance was put in place, nothing! I know what you're thinking. I know you think I was just some terrible troublemaker, right? Then you haven't been listening very well. I wasn't that kid. To know me was to know I cared, yes—fun, energetic, free-spirited—!...But I cared, and wanted to do the right thing. I didn't reside in drama-filled environments or looking-for-trouble teenage pastimes. At school, I was the perfect student. As long as I could have sports, poetry, good friends, and company with laughter, I was good! But come on people. I was the youngest of 7—did you hear?! Knowing how to stand toe to toe with anyone that threatened my being became 2$^{nd}$ nature. Of course, eventually, I defended myself against the constant bullies I had to face, but I was not the culprit. Ask about me! LOL.

So here I am—walking the 'lavish' halls of a predominately white Christian school. Apostolic at that! I was exposed to a whole different group of people AND worshiped from a different angle. This could have been considered a season of planting—sowing seeds—in me, a time for a new direction.

Even my writings during this time were changing. What helped me fall in love with poetry was how inviting and safe she was—I could express my hopefulness, my joys, my triumphs, and at the same time, my isolation, my sadness, and all its colors, my tears, my fears, even my dreams—all without negative input or judgment. Poetry was my haven. My beau! Instead of these poems happening during feel-good highs, they came at very quiet, pensive lows.

I started talking to God more. I felt like I was getting to know Him for myself and not just what I had been taught. Despite some changing thought patterns, I wasn't a finished masterpiece; I was still engaging in my *escape* methods. At the time, I didn't know how else to deal with the hurt; the reality was too loud. I didn't want to face that pain, and I don't think I even believed I could. I thought it would break me—thought I would lose what was left of me. Sad thing was I'd grown agonizingly tired of pretending to be strong. After living in a situation for so long, it has a way of taking ownership, and without notice—you've surrendered control. Women, especially African American women, are strong because no one gave them permission not to be, or allowed them to feel safe enough not to be, and for the 1% this doesn't apply to—congrats! That's how insidious dysfunction is…you don't see it coming until it's all over you. Hence, our strength can become our greatest weakness if it isn't handled in a healthy manner. I had this weird feeling like God was trying to get a message through to me, yet I couldn't unscramble the words.

Like Morse code with no interpretation. Now, instead of talking to my dad, I began talking to my Father…*wink* did y'all catch that though? When I was alone in my room, I could release all the pressure to God. So, I did. I clothed him with my burdened heart so He could take some of the weight off of me. Talking to God never made me feel like less of a person. In a weird way, I felt whole in those moments. He didn't judge me or dismantle me like people can with the preconceived ideas, notions, and judgmental conclusions that they carry. Somehow, within the midst of my *chaotic* life, I knew one day God would pick me up and carry me away—lift me from under the mess that was contaminating who I was meant to be. It may be a physical lift, or it may only be a spiritual, emotional, or mental lift; either way, I needed Him to lift me. It was that belief that told me to hold on…

So yes, I was dealing with a lot internally—don't say I didn't warn y'all. I said, "dive into the vast corridors of my deepest, remembered memories…" so what were you expecting? Huh?! I know, it was a lot—but hey, on another note, I am 16 now! Let's talk about that nice driver's license, or how about that Ford F-150. Yassss, honey! My first vehicle was a beautiful, midnight blue Ford F-150. Please know, I used to whip that thang. Mind you, my poor baby already had a few bangs and dents from that one time…what? Oh, I didn't tell you? I thought I mentioned the time my dad picked me up from school and was already sitting in the passenger seat when I came out.

Awww shoot! He's about to let me drive home. Wait! I don't have on my glasses. *(Author inserts dramatic sigh)* For my readers that do not know me personally, first off, hello, thank you for buying my book...ok, ok, but just so you know, I'm almost blind. Like, not actually, but really close. I've been wearing glasses since I was 7. So, the story goes like this. I didn't have my glasses on because they were broken. They were broken because—uhhh, I broke them! They hadn't been replaced yet because my mom said I would have to replace them myself. After all, she was over buying new glasses *(wait for it, here comes the hyperbole)* every time she turned around. Really, mom?! I mean, I had only gone through—what, like, 3 or 4 pairs. That wasn't too bad. Yeah, right! Valeria wasn't going, honey. So, I was in the process of saving up for my new glasses when I walked out of the school to find my dad sitting in the passenger seat! Whyyyyyyyy?! I'm 16 people. There was no way I was going to turn this down, duh! SO—I did what any teen would do. I rationalized with myself. I know the way home like the back of my hand. As long as we go home, I don't have to see crystal clear. Right? WRONG! Y'all, we get to driving down University Dr., and as we approach MLK Blvd., Dad says keep straight. Huh? What ya say? Come again, say what? Keep straight, you said? Panic is setting in— help! Stay calm, E. You got this—girl, stop lying, you don't got this. Tell this man, you can't see. Too late, I'm driving. Tell him! No, I got this! Ok, so I went with the left-shoulder devil. "No problem, Dad," I say with poise. Picture this—he wants to go to

Home Depot, which I now know is on Orchard Lake…but then, maaan, ion *(yes, I said "ion" instead of I don't)* know how to get to no Home Depot. What do y'all think I did? Yup, sure did— pretended like I knew. I put my confidence on, and thankfully, traffic wasn't too heavy. That way, I could drive slow enough to allow time to react, but fast enough not to look blind. I almost made it, y'all. We're still on University Dr.—ok, there's In and Out, there's that park I used to play at, there's Shiloh Church—I know this street. Dad is quietly observing me. I must be doing good, he ain't said much. Cool! Let's roll. I crossed over Paddock—it was a green light, no issues there. Then, the light, the corner, and the turn lane that burst my bubble wide open—Wide Track, A.K.A., The Loop! Now known as Woodward Ave. There was a right-turn-only lane, and a keep-straight or turn lane. Well, readers, because Dad hadn't said or given any directions, my assumption was to keep straight. That's good logic, don't you think? Problem with my logic was that I didn't take into account that I couldn't see, and therefore hadn't noticed that I was in the right-turn-only lane. I'm sitting at this red light, boldly waiting for green so I can keep straight because Daddy ain't said nothing about no turning. Little side note for those not familiar with Pontiac. The reason Daddy hadn't said anything is because you could literally get to Orchard Lake, ya know, where Home Depot was, either way. Clearly, he thought I was turning because that's what you do when you're in a right-turn-only lane. He had no reason to believe what happened next was even possible. That man was in the passenger seat, chilling y'all. My green light arrives, and—oh boy! I kept straight. Now, hear me out, reader. Don't come for me! If there were no traffic, this would have easily been a teachable moment. Dad would have seen I didn't turn and could ask, "Why, daughter?"—to which I could then respond and be honest about not knowing where I was going—and not being able to see. I mean, work with me people. But no, there was traffic, so none of that even matters. As I confidently kept straight to cross over Wide Track, the car to my left—in the keep-straight or turn lane—was turning right (and rightfully so), completely destroyed my delusional smooth transition towards Perry St.—Boom! Pow! Crack! Pop! WHAT IS HAPPENING?! Abort, abort! I've been hit. Ship is sinking! I was too scared to even react. With my 10 & 2 driving skills, I pulled over to the side of the road, put the car in park, and looked at my dad for answers while trying to breathe. I think I forgot how to breathe. "Are you ok?" asked Dad. "Yes, I think so," I responded. Dad got out and dealt with the damages. Now you know why my beautiful, midnight blue, Ford F-150 had dimples. May I have your attention, please? We will now proceed to the next chapter. There is no need for y'all to go on laughing at me the way you are right now. Enough is enough! Check, please!

## SHADOWING LYRICS OF MY LIFE

*All my life, I've wanted someone, somebody—to truly understand the person within.*

*Only look beyond the outer appearance and see the thoughts behind the pen.*

*To love and not know how to clearly express the beauty of your happiness—is like being incarcerated inside yourself.*

*Locked away, and no one has the key.*

*It seems as though I've always aimed at the wrong things.*

*Striving to do right, instead of just doing right.*

*His love dictates my soul and takes my fears away—it lets me see light in the midst of the night.*

*Sometimes, life feels like an endless storm—with each wave, I think of what might, could, or should happen—never just letting go of the wheel—saying yes to His will.*

*My dreams seem so real, yet I still land as a skeptic.*

*Can this really be so? Does He—with understanding—actually know?*

*Who I am, what I feel, what I'm saying in the absence of words...*

*All I want in life will never amount to what He's already given me.*

*His love was so great that He gave all of His life for mine.*

*And now, with but one way—I am drifted by the same wave.*

*I am carried by the same arms, happy from the same joy, understood by the same mind.*

*And loved with only one love!*

## POETIC SYMPHONY

*My pen to this paper is like gifted fingers on an old piano. The words that lift from my lines have a musical, rhythmic tune, like the aesthetic sound of a 3-part harmony.*

*This is my poetic symphony...*

*The intricate process of my thoughts as they diligently seek to be transformed into spoken word is like the mind of an orchestrator while he conducts the violin and the flute—the organ and the bass. Many pieces, one puzzle.*

*There is symmetry, truth, and expression—it is truly a euphony.*

*This is my poetic symphony...*

*I admire these words in the way Kind David played the harp, in the way he danced until he was despised. It's an inner sound that sometimes the artist can only find.*

*I feel my words like a choir preparing for the next octave, lifting their eyes and hands in anticipation.*

*I respect poetry for her honesty—honest like the 10-year-old soprano whose voice is unafraid to explore its range—cracks and all.*

*It's an inner melody.*

*This is my poetic symphony...*

*So, pull my strings, blow my horn, and beat my drum.*

*Poetry is making music to my spirit—I am alive.*

*This is my poetic symphony...singing just for me.*

## NIGHT ROAR

*At night, when the dark sky is high,*

*His wondrous works make me sigh.*

*As I grow nigh—I want to cry.*

*The night roar triggers the question, what for?*

*And I want to know more.*

*My heart is flaming with fire—Jesus is truly higher!*

*My soul yearns to be the one He loves.*

*Lifting my mind with wings, I soar high like the doves!*

*Shooting star, shining moon's glow.*

*With me in mind, and now I know.*

*It's mine—and at night, I share in the beauty*

*Of knowing He knew me.*

## BEAUTIFULLY JUST ME

*I'm tired of wondering when I laugh, is it annoying to this person or that person.*

*I'm tired of caring whether they were talking about me.*

*I'm tired of suppressing the way I am, and more importantly, who I am!*

*Previously, this has been spoken, however, I've concluded that when situations repeat themselves, a lesson is hanging nearby, waiting for me to learn.*

*I must've missed it 'cause this topic has resurfaced.*

*And God says, "this time, pay attention."*

*I want to be carefree, like Jessica Simpson, with nothing but a t-shirt on.*

*I want to lay back in the trees like the Koala that hasn't a care in the world.*

*I want to laugh like I ain't got no backbone.*

*Laughing like Julia Roberts in Pretty Woman when she got paid...*

*Like Shug Avery in Color Purple when she called Celie, ugly.*

*I want to be me in the way I was meant to be.*

*I want to express myself in a way that's uniquely me.*

*Beautifully just me!*

*I like the way my laugh makes my stomach muscles tight—it's a good workout!*

*I like the way I find the smallest things to smile about when others think I'm crazy.*

*'Cause they can't see what I see the way I see it!*

*I like the way I'm vibrant—'cause why not?*

*I am outgoing! I am energetic! I am vivacious!*

*I am beautifully just me!*

*I want to laugh like Erinn Imari—'cause that's me!*

*Beautifully just me!*

## GOD IS MY STRENGTH

*God is my strength when I am weak.*

*He is always there to hear me speak.*

*When I am down, He lifts me up.*

*And when that time comes, at His table, I will sup.*

*Only in Him do I trust, for He is Lord of all!*

*His promises are ever true—He will uphold my fall.*

*God is my strength through night and day.*

*He is in my heart, and there He will stay!*

## WHY I LOVE HER

*I didn't think I could want her anymore than I already do. She's so sweet to me! I love her softness and the smell of her presence—mouth-watering, instant gratifying attraction.*

*Truly tongue-tied experiences—perfect satisfaction!*

*She's so sweet to me! Cold or warm…it doesn't matter too much; she's good at anytime.*

*By herself or joined by another—hmm, cherries on top will go even further.*

*She's lovely with a chocolate kiss—I desire for her to touch my lips.*

*She's deliciously, dynamic; passionately, pleasing; and simply succulent!*

*She's so sweet to me! Staring me in my face, I promise none will go to waste.*

*With just the right pace, trust me…*

*Cheesecake is the perfect taste…She's so sweet to me!*

## LET THOSE THAT HAVE EARS

*Look into my eyes like an open door, and you will see that I'm trying to explore.*

*Why do my people continue to look to this world for answers and are oblivious to the fact that their knees should be on the floor, head up, and eyes toward the Lord?*

*Now, my intention was not to get too deep—sometimes, though, when you allow His mind, this mind to be in you, things are spoken, and words are heard that, when placed in this supernatural order, don't seem so absurd.*

*If you ask me, what really needs to be done is an awakening on the inside, cause it's the inside that needs to come out on the outside so that our lights can truly shine.*

*But no, my people perish for lack of knowledge, and with it standing directly in our faces, we don't even know how to acknowledge it—Yet we do know how to curse one another; we do know how to condemn and condescend.*

*We even know how to professionally kick someone with the right geometric angle, and in the right position—when they're already down.*

*If I opened up Ephesians and told you that there should be an exhortation to unity,*

*That if we spoke the truth in love, we would begin to grow up.*

*I would tell you how we are one body, one people, one nation, and that effectually working together, we produce fruit and increase for the body—We edify...this is building one another in love.*

*And like my pastor always says, it takes a mature believer to read Ephesians, so I hope I haven't made anyone choke—but these generational curses need to be broken.*

*And I told yall I wasn't trying to go too deep.*

*Consequently, some of yall may need to revert back to the milk cause this mountain may be a little too steep—and you still trying to climb the rough side—when God simply told you to speak!*

*See, these words I'm speaking were given by inspiration, and if we were being led like we're supposed to, our children wouldn't be rebelling and searching for the affection*

*Momma tries to give, yet it's wanted from Daddy, but Daddy can't give—See, Daddy's been on that stuff for some time now.*

*If we were being led like we're supposed to—we wouldn't have bipolar, schizophrenia, and depression disorders. If we were being led—there would be no sickness and disease, poverty and lack. If we were being led...I know that by His stripes, we are healed...I know His will for us is health and prosperity. I know He said no good thing would He withhold if we delighted in Him.*

*However, it seems nowadays that these are just churchy cliches. The world promises a lifetime of pleasures, but the end is eternal damnation. The joyride won't last forever.*

*It only increases your sinful trophy collection.*

*Oh, taste and see! See and taste—oh, that the Lord is good!*

*Don't you know that we are meant to be Egyptian kings and Nubian queens walking in authority, living life without apology?*

*Understand that I don't have to pick up a .45 to kill; I can speak idle words and dispatch angels that are not from above—and without a bullet I just took away life.*

*Faith comes by hearing, hearing God's word.*

*Life comes by speaking, speaking God's word.*

*Let no corrupt communication proceed out of your mouth, but that which is good to the use of edifying, that it may minister grace unto the hearers. Can you hear?*

## TEARS OF SORROW

*I can't seem to understand why I can't have you.*

*I've done everything in my power to get you close to me.*

*I stood by your side even when you'd done me the worst.*

*There were times that you treated me so cruelly and yet,*

*I was still there, waiting for you to just want me too.*

*You told me so many times that you cared and loved me.*

*Deep down inside, I knew you cared.*

*By your actions, though, I knew you couldn't love me true.*

*I gave you my all, and you were my world.*

*In return, you gave me nothing.*

*I knew it would take time for the pain to heal.*

*After the love, the dreams, and the happiness,*

*It was just too hard to say good-bye.*

*Seems strange, but at times I envisioned,*

*You were next to me when I slept.*

*It then was the only way I could fall asleep.*

*Does love hurt?*

*I guess what is meant is meant—what isn't, just isn't.*

*I can finally say I'm not confused anymore.*

*It would've been great to see you every morning,*

*When I opened my eyes.*

*But now, I'm doing what I should have done yesterday,*

*Saying good-bye sorrow.*

## THE GENTLE TOUCH

*At times, I feel a chill—tingles I feel.*

*It's like going downhill—my heart starts to unravel and peel.*

*I close my eyes—and You appear!*

*But is it really You that I hear?*

*That gentle touch soothes my aching soul.*

*It fills my spirit with joy—your voice is one of a kind!*

*I hope it's real—not just in my mind.*

*And as the night grows high—the stars are in the sky.*

*Oh—I know it's not a fallacy because I actually feel You*

*Growing nigh.*

## A CALL FOR BEAUTY

*Exposed—my weaknesses are exposed—the helplessness shows...Every ugly thing I try to cover is on display. I ask myself, how do I even know what's pure in me and what's not?*

*He that has clean hands and a pure heart.*

*Inadequate, incomplete, not enough, partial—my inabilities, my proclivities, it wasn't me.*

*I'm insufficient, see—me! How do I escape me?! I'm nothing! What is my mere existence that it should be counted as a matter of value? I'm full of evil...living and growing on the inside since birth—taking root in the forest of pleasure and sinful plays—using me as a host, draining my worth—Increasing the body count, my soul dismayed—no, I'm not a serial killer, but because of me, look at the souls not saved.*

*I can't survive the glory of the Holy God. Exalted, yet gracious! Sovereign, but patient! Almighty, yet merciful—the Lion and the Lamb! Who am I that the Great I AM would combine deity with humanity, shamefully clothe Himself with sin and endure the cross?*

*The Great I AM, allowing the epitome of Earth's scum to spit on Him, beat Him—to disfigurement...and still He prayed, Father, forgive them.*

*The Great I AM—looked in me—naked and unclothed—and His blood came streaming down—took His life that I may be; loved and never forsaken—pierced His side—out of my belly shall flow rivers of living water—and then, gave up the Ghost...on His own*

*Yes, His life, no man can take it!*

*So like my Boss on the cross, I submit to God's will—I say have Your way God and do what You will—Mold me, I'm still on the Potter's wheel—Gut me, take out all the bad stuff...the stuff you can't use, it's spoiled and with it I lose.*

*Make me beautiful—give me beauty for these ashes that I've carried far too long.*

*Make me beautiful—yes me!*

*Make me beautiful—the miracle of imminent grace yesterday, today, and forever.*

*Make me beautiful—align every organ, cell, and tissue that it operates according to the order when You spoke life into me—and it was good!*

*Make me beautiful—Make me beautiful—wounds and all, perfectly marred—take even my scars—*

*Make me beautiful—Make me more like You.*

## *THANK YOU*

*As emotions want to erupt,*

*I feel a weakening inside.*

*Each time my tear ducts swell, I distract them with another thought.*

*I'm learning that sometimes I just gotta tough it out.*

*Telling myself to praise right now, at this very moment, seems harder than steel.*

*I know though, that if I can just get a thank-you out, the rest will flow.*

*Lord, be Thou my help!*

*In the midst of this, when every turn, the enemy surrounds,*

*Be Thou my protection, my shield.*

*I open up my word for encouragement, and as I let out a sigh, I close my eyes and say, thank you!*

## CONFOUNDING THE WISE

*As I sit, contemplating, wondering why.*

*I say to myself, I must rely—on the everlasting arms of the Most*

*High! And realize—He's the light in my eyes.*

*That forces me to push—and push—and push!*

*Oh, even those times when I feel I can't go on.*

*I know I must be strong!*

*The veracity of His words will precisely cause perplexity.*

*If you try comprehension from an infant level of mentality,*

*Pay attention to the reality.*

*Are you promised the next second, minute, or hour?*

*I don't remember the last time you made the sun rise—besides…*

*Is life or death determined in your hands?—or did I mistakenly*

*conclude that you're a man, or woman?*

*Whether reception is taken on your part or not—it's there.*

*And it needs to be clear—His coming is near!*

*Having empathy for your ignorance yet understanding it's not*

*equal to innocence intending no offense—when will this world*

*come to grips?*

*That He's the Almighty, Prince of Peace, King of kings, and Lord*

*of lords! That came to die for your sins.*

*Even though you were worthless—try not to fall into the trends.*

*My prayers are intercession—hoping for your confession,*

*That will lead you to a revelation of His manifestation.*

*America, God has blessed you tremendously.*

*Now enormously, bless God!*

# VOLUME 4

Brandy is coming to Detroit! I was in love with her and Monica at this time in my life. This is why siblings are your first best friends. My sister and her boyfriend, at the time, now husband, surprised me with concert tickets for my birthday to go see Brandy. Whaaaat! Do you even understand how excited I was? It goes without saying that I had to be fly; gotta call my bestie and tell her all about it, and gotta write 3 pages in my diary about the whole experience. Since it was my first concert, we shouldn't be surprised that I was star- struck immediately. Did my girl just come up from the ground? Did she just jump into the crowd and let them catch her? Is she really singing *The Boy is Mine* right in front of me? Is she really singing all the songs from my favorite album, *Never Say Never?* I'm having the time of my life. I look to my left, and my sister is up dancing too. What a moment! I knew every song on that album like I had written them myself. Those songs felt like my poetry. They said everything I was feeling and some. I would sing these songs in the shower like I was in concert. They played in the background while I cleaned. I hummed them while doing homework. I mean, really related to her artistry. *Have You Ever* was set on repeat, and poems about my knight in shining armor were passionately etched in ink from its inspiration.

I guess by now, I was so deeply in love with my knight in shining armor, it didn't matter that it wasn't an authentic relationship. Telling me I was too young to know real love—went in one ear and out the other. I just knew, as do *all* we females, that

I was with my husband. Perfect was he not, but it never seemed to deter my mind. He loved me; at least, that's what he said. So, I believed him, or so I told myself I did. It was what I needed at that time, what I longed for. If we're honest with ourselves, it's very possible that what we think is best for us and the things we desire most are the very things keeping us from the best thing for us and blocking our sincerest desires from being realized. Sometimes, the haze, the fog, the familiar is just easier. No? Oh, maybe that was just me. Back to the story…he was a *good* distraction from life inside my house. I had some other distractions too, but none quite as special as he. See, I needed the distractions from him too. How long can a person pretend before losing it?! There were still pieces of my heart that hadn't fully healed since he shattered it—that night—in the basement. These distractions were pain inhibitors that helped to mask the hurt he had created. I knew he didn't love me. Not like I loved him. Come on now! I knew! He had my heart though, the broken pieces and those that were still together, whether he wanted it or not. I'm just being honest. Y'all, I was so caught up in this boy that his wrongs, how he treated me, and the other girls were simply not an issue. I just made those doses of reality go poof—disappear. It seemed easier that way—to just pretend like I was his only. Like, I was the one he dreamt about and the one he took home to meet his mama. If only walls had ears to hear and a mouth to talk—listening to me rant and rave about my future ideal world with him. Yeah, my family didn't have a clue—all those years that I wanted love and affection and wasn't getting it at home, I was giving it to him—all my immature ideas and naiveté about love…were shared with him. Because I was in the mess, from that viewpoint, I couldn't see anything else. This altered reality was much easier to accept than the hell that was *my life*.

My mama didn't raise me to be a fool. I was very precocious and intuitive—bold personality. Very bright, to say the least—so I had been told. I may not have been getting the tender love I felt so deprived of, but it didn't blind me from seeing Mama as a strong woman. Mama didn't take any jive from anyone. I watched how she interacted with others—how skilled and intelligent she was with what she said. Mama had class, and she was so elegant and smooth. I learned how to exude confidence just by seeing it in her, yet when it came to this one boy, my intelligent composure failed me every time. How could I be so blind to him? I was a good student, an athlete, a student council member, an honor student at that—lacking brains was just not it. Earnestly, I craved the endorphins his smile could bring. Seeing me in school or away from my home was like seeing a different person all together. I smiled and laughed—I hugged like it was my long-lost friend as often as I could. If you didn't look beyond the surface, you missed my tears. That's why I loved my knight so much. I created a place in my mind for him. I erased all the bad, and when I was with him—no rain, no clouds, I only saw sunshine.

Eventually, that fairytale of mine began to fade. For no particular reason, I started noticing things about this boy. There comes a time when the Spirit breaks through the noise and speaks—and you finally hear. I began having those same feelings of abandonment I experienced at home with him. Less and less time he would have for me. More and more excuses of why he had to call me back. "Naw, not today, I'll talk to you later," he'd say. My suspicions were growing, and for no apparent reason. You know that feeling that you just can't shake, yet you don't know why? Now, after all this time, I actually cared that I wasn't his only girl. Oh, but the summer came. And it was the summer before my senior year! Oh, yes, my loves—I met someone that summer. I know it's easy to read these lines and think, this girl is crazy in love with this boy—and I was. But I told y'all…something wasn't right, and I wasn't passing up my chances to have a good time waiting on him. It's a warm and sunny day, and I'm at an open house. Some people call it a graduation party. I hardly know any of these people, but my bestie had asked me to go with her, so I went. Next thing I know, I'm being asked can I go to pick somebody up in my beautiful, midnight blue, Ford F-150. I was not eager to do that, but I told my bestie, sure I'll go, but that she had to come with me. I pull up at the corner house, and here he comes. Looking like a tall glass of water on this sun-shiny day. He gets in my car like he just knows me. Uh, "hi," I say as he flashes that dimple at me. It was hard to keep my composure. Wow—was my first impression…he's breath-taking. Instantly, I noticed he was totally different from my knight. Tall, browned skin, football-body, built—hmm. He intrigued me. He had something I wanted, but I didn't know what it was. I drive us back to the party, and I remember just getting lost in watching him. I was smitten. He was so charismatic, sociable, genuine, and funny—and apparently, he thought I was too cause he laughed at all my corny comments.

The time went by, and now the party is over. He walks over to me and says, "am I riding back home with you?" "Yeah, I'll take you home," I say, as I put in overtime effort to stay calm. "What's your name again?" he asked. "Erinn" I reply, shyly. "Can I call you sometime?" slides out his mouth. "Ok, here's my number, (248) 335-5007," I barely manage to utter. Since my knight didn't have time for me, I enjoyed the fact that someone else did. This guy was a little older than me. I thought to myself— ooh—he's experienced. I drive off, screaming all the way to the light, "bestie, *who dis man, Harpo?*" Why had she never told me about him—hello! Call me crazy, I know it's too soon, but he was my four-leaf clover—rare! He made me feel right on special too. It was that new kind of special though. Y'all, this man was smooth. The way he could put words together, spin them, connect them—déjà vu—like my mirror image. Who sent him? "Uh, excuse me, sir, who sent you?" is what I should've asked. He seemed interested in Erinn and not her façade or what she could give him. He saw her—and accepted her. Whoa! We became so close in such a short time. He was an adrenaline rush all on his own. He fed my smiles without even trying. He accepted my eccentric personality and behavior as if it was all he'd ever known. I had never experienced anything or anyone like him. I wanted to study him, dissect him—who sent you? I felt like I had already known him and had just forgotten. Our conversations were so full of life and energetic. Long walks with nowhere to go—finishing each other's sentences—connected, gelled together like peas and carrots (in my Forrest Gump voice). Writing songs and poetry together—embracing and respecting the art and skill we had both honed. Like, my knight never cared about my poetry. Did he even know I wrote? One random night stands out to me. We're walking back towards our side of town, coming from a friend's house. For no reason, he asks me, "do you trust me?" I say, "yes" with no hesitation. "Close your eyes," he whispers. I did. "I'm going to guide you with my words, and you can't peek." he instructs. I didn't. Are y'all getting this? It's dark outside! Am I nuts, or what? We still have a long way to walk—but I trusted him, and I didn't even know why. I don't think I've ever given someone, me, the way I gave me to him. This is that stuff you read about in a romance novel. This doesn't happen in real life…but it did. So, with my eyes closed and literally not peeking, I let his voice guide me passed the rocks and dips, curbs and sticks—all the way to the front door. I opened my eyes as he announces, "we're here." I'm sorry, but that was deep. So deep, it scared me. He was becoming my best friend. I trusted him—with me, the one most people didn't know. Like, I could depend on him to love and care for me the way I wanted to love and care for me. Genuinely! Sadly, summer had to end. My friend and his dimple left to go back from whence they came, and I had to return to my reality.

Then, it happened! The news that destroyed my heart, tornado style—I mean, it traumatized me to the bone. Something inside me, burst—ruptured! I had this saying, "If she can take him, he was never mine." It was a mindset more than anything. If a man could leave you for someone else, then what you believed about the relationship was not the true version of the story. So it goes in life, be careful of the attachments you form and allow. Everything we allow ourselves to become attached to isn't to our benefit. Leeches come to do one thing—take! Anyhoo, I don't know why this time was so different, but the news and evidence had been placed at my feet that my knight in shining armor had been with somebody else. I don't know if it was the details she knew or specific dates she could recollect; I don't know if it was the comfort with which she described their interactions or if it was the fact that her name was not on that list of girls he'd been with. He didn't mention her. Why? The ones I knew of, I thought that hurt, but this hurt me to the core. I actually knew this girl! I know. I know what you're thinking. I wasn't his special girl, anyway. But again, we're talking about my point of view, keep up people. I was in love, ok! Yes—I knew just like he knew that it was only *my* fantasy for us to live happily ever after. This time though, it didn't just break my heart, it broke me. Something on the inside stopped working—died! All my trust, all my smiles, and all my beliefs of happiness were wrapped up in this boy. And just like that—it was ripped away from my grasp. His alleyway adventures had come to the light, and I was lost in the shadow of it all. Senses disoriented. Wholeheartedly torn. Broken.

Physically speaking, when your eyes water, your tear ducts are operating on a normal basis to lubricate and protect the eye. When you have an emotion, brain signals are sent, causing the ducts to overact, and it creates tears—this is crying. When the emotions become so strong, so intense, your brain tells your tear ducts to release the surplus water. Your body doesn't want to contain them. So why do we keep them in the way we do? Sometimes, your body just needs to weep. To release what it doesn't need. These emotions needed to come out. They were too powerful for me to hold in…my mind and my senses were in autopilot, but I had no clue of what to do or how to fix it. It was affecting me more than I could have expected. My days were quietly dry as I bathed in the melancholy aroma of a fragmented heart chopped into more pieces.   Even though I had stopped talking to my knight, my mind wouldn't stop the memories. Sadness set on replay like a grenade of regret exploding with every tear that fell. I lay heavily in bed at night, smoking my cigs and crying myself to sleep—thinking *where did I go wrong? What did I not do—what did I not give? God, what are you doing to my life?* My grades were slipping—my *escape* methods were no escape. I drank just to fall asleep and still, only to awaken to the same pain—the same dull throbbing within the pit of my stomach. A hangover would have offered more relief than this. No one noticed. No day seemed any different in our house. No behavior was worth a second glance. Emotional and psychological concerns were not a topic of discussion. I no longer tried as hard to get the attention I still secretly and desperately craved at home. Things had settled with my dad, but nothing was the same. Somehow, I knew it was never going to be. We were getting to know one another in spite of how much it had changed. In good ways and bad. I mean, it was Daddy who greeted me every time I was sneaking back into the house. Yup! He got me every time. Even if I wasn't learning the new him, he was surely learning me, alright. I had developed some skills at this point, though—or so I thought. My lying wasn't the best, but I still told it. I did my chores and didn't bother anyone, didn't ask for much. I let go of caring about whether they cared about me or not. I made myself believe that. Even though I knew I still cared…a lot more than I knew how to admit. In my mind, the sooner I could get away—the better. So, I gave in…I let my body weep—and that it did. I wept! You ever cried for months?

## YOU TOLD ME

*I'm tired of love. I'm tired of the void it leaves—I gotta let it go.*

*I take the blame because I shoulda left a long time ago, after 1, 2, 3, and 4 second chances...It's sad because I stayed around and tried to make it work.*

*Turned my head at the questionable situations, the obvious flirtations. Gave you time to sort your thoughts—time to get yourself together.*

*Winter, Spring, Summer, Fall—I've seen them all, yet I waited. I waited—dated here and there, but my heart waited. It waited...*

*Waited because you told me if I were there, you'd choose me— waited because you told me you would come here for me. Waited because you told me you wanted me to be your only girl. I guess my time just expired—*

*while I was forgiving every "oops baby, I'm sorry,"*

*years were being taken from me, and the reason behind my longing simply became fantasy.*

*I gave you enough—you almost walked off with all my stuff.*

*I've heard it said, don't give it all because in the end, all that's left is bitterness and regret. But I don't regret making sure that you were always ok—*

*Did you eat, boo? Are you hungry? Do you need to be alone? You need anything, baby?*

*I don't regret it at all.*

*Sometimes, however, I wonder, was it worth it...ion know!*

*I'm not mad—just tired of love. I gotta let that ish go!*

*And yeah, I did wait—and for what?*

*All good—now I'm doing the forsaking—my wait is over and goodbye is in the making.*

*Prized possession over this way baby—for the man who's ready— he's determined, motivated, and dedicated to what it takes to keep a good woman by his side.*

*See, all along I was waiting for you, but I know you'll soon realize, I was that spark behind your eyes, the one who tied your ties, listened to all your cries, endured all the tries to compromise.*

*Campbell's Chicken Noodle Soup, Vick's Vapor Rub too—I was the one who stood by your side, a helping hand I did provide. What happened boo, you told me I would be your bride—the warmth against your chest, the one you named the best from all the rest— the laughter behind your genuine smile, willing to walk the longest mile—'cause you told me*

*It would be worth my while.*

*I thought it made me complete, but Vivian Green reminded me…*

*Truth is—all those things you told me, you can do me a fovor and save ya statement…*

*I'm complete without it.*

## TICK TOCK

*How much longer will I let the time slip away?*

*We are never promised the next day.*

*Thus, we must live each day, as if it were on purpose,*

*Thrusting out the potential.*

*So many times we've told ourselves…and others,*

*It can wait until tomorrow.*

*Well, tomorrow came, and is now gone.*

*Sometimes, tomorrow doesn't come at all.*

*So do we lose the moment to seize all it brings?*

*Or do we take it and go for it?*


*God tells us that He will always be there.*

*But this day won't always be here.*

*And stubbornly, we don't look at that aspect.*

*Because as usual, we suspect.*

*We've got all the time in the world.*

*Not only do we not have forever,*

*We also don't know.*

*In the blink of an eye, it could just be gone.*

*We're left alone.*

*There's no one there to console.*

*There's no more time left.*

*But oh no, it was only yesterday.*


*Tick Tock, time just ran out!*

## HOW COME

*Tell me why they flow?*

*These tears—I can't make them stop.*

*Why are they here?*

*I still feel him at times when he's not even there.*

*I'm hurting—my aching heart, it yearns to be filled.*

*I try and I try. Friends ask me why*

*He's no good for you they tell me.*

*But…I guess I choose to hurt again.*

*But I don't want to hurt again.*

*I don't want sleepless, lonely nights.*

*Waking up in cold sweats, holding my pillow extra tight.*

*All I want is for him to love me back.*

*I desire for his touch to be as sincere as the ocean's blue.*

*Soft like a baby that's brand new.*

*He convinced me yall, said baby, it's me and you.*

*I've loved him for so long,*

*To just stop—it doesn't seem right.*

*I can't walk away—I love him.*

*Too much and too hard—I love him.*

*He's all I know—he's all I have.*

*He is my smile. He's my warmth inside cold thoughts,*

*The sparkle that beams from my left eye.*

*He's the truth that reveals any lie.*

*But a bleeding heart do I have?*

*Cause I can't seem to tell him, goodbye.*

## IN MY MIND

*Cold, winter chills, emotionally blazing into summer nights,*

*Remembering the sweat rolling down my brow,*

*I may not have walked the steps myself, but I was there,*

*In my mind..*

*I can see the skin rise with disfigurement—the body jerk from*

*relentless pain,*

*Blow after blow,*

*I may not have walked the steps myself, but I was there,*

*In my mind...*

*The path gets longer with each lift of the foot...Fingers become*

*numb and burned from the sun's glare. The blood...oh the blood—*

*it runs down my face settling into the cracks, engraved in my skin.*

*My vision is blurred, my hearing impaired,*

*I may not have walked the steps myself, but I was there,*

*In my mind..*

*(sing)    Wade in the water, wade in the water, children, wade...*

*I hold my head up as the tears begin to wash away the dried stains*

*upon my cheeks...I lift my hands up and I rise—this is an obstacle*

*I shall survive.*

*My people will not be depleted—this journey has already been*

*stampeded.*

*By the screams and moans of the oppressed—stampeded by the*

*unyielding fire within...they pressed—this journey has already*

*been stampeded.*

*On the back of my Savior, hanging and dying, He still said—for you I did it.*

*This journey has already been completed.*

*So I walk it.*

*I will walk down the narrow road and sing the story as if its never been told.*

*Because I may not have walked the steps myself, but I was there, In my mind..*

*We are more than conquerors—we win!*

*In the end—we win!*

*So I wear my crown—'cause…In my mind…why not?!*

## HIDDEN WOUNDS

*I feel like I'm in defense mode...gratifying my flesh.*

*I know this, but I'd rather blow him a kiss, hope that I won't be missed, that my name makes it on that list.*

*Denying, evading, rationalizing all the truths that swarm my mind, in order to keep my emotions blind.*

*I stay hidden, off to the side, declined if you will... yet attesting to be defined.*

*I tell you, man, I'm completely entwined—in the nothingness of my numbness.*

*The voice that never stops calling, the door that will always keep drumming, the answers that forever keep coming...alive...inside my mind, but confined to the beat of my pleasure rhyme. Head tilted down, brutal truth is*

*I'm lost inside these soulish wounds and even though it seems I've come out, scars have formed—at night...yea at night. Triggered by the smallest acts, I plead with me, not to react...*

*Reading, singing, dancing, braiding—nothing truly distracts, washing, crying, lying in my bed—Gone? No, it's closer than I want to admit. I quit...I quit wanting it. Stopped embracing it, giving it credibility no more. Yet when and how do I really get legit?*

*I have escaped reality and ran fiercely toward the fallacy. I'm tangled in this maze so deep, so thick, too quick.*

*I swear I'm not this chick, but the game was so slick...*

*and I had been out for so long...drastic was this pick—one night, one ride, one whiff of his scent and I was carsick.*

*This man became my righteous accent, and I was his sidekick...weak—love potions declared.*

*Now here, hesitantly I sit, embarking upon a new season, a new page to turn, and I struggle to face me...as if, afraid of who I might see—wondering how many times can one be set free? How long before I am truly ready...when it's no longer maybe and I'm not going crazy?*

*Writing to no end, no conclusion to contend—my fingers usher in comfort with each stroke of my pen.*

*I remember back when, but then, once again...all over again.*

## MY FIRST KISS WITH HIM

*Gazing into his stare—I could see his thoughts.*

*I could feel his heart skip, jump—uh oh…did it just stop?*

*Flirtatious acts, switching hips—*

*Yet, covered in style, I couldn't seem to place my lips against this.*

*Tall and slim, sunset on a warm night, chunk of a sexy black man's lips.*

*How luscious and sensual they do appear?*

*As if I would have drifted into paradise,*

*Here he comes…getting closer.*

*Now I'm nervous.*

*I closed my eyes as I visualized—my MOM!*

*No, girl! Not Mama!*

*Ok—there it is.*

*I see blue waterfalls, jasmine flowers, and candlelit walls of love.*

*I couldn't turn back now.*

*But is now the right time?*

*How—When? Wait a minute—rewind.*

*I just watched Midnight Love on BET.*

*I can do this. I'm a Sistah, a strong Sistah, at that!*

*Boy, are you ready for me?*

*I opened my eyes, grasped his face, and pulled him in.*

*Passions exploded from left to right inside my body.*

*Is it safe to feel this way? Dang boo, let's do it again!*

## LOVE SO REAL

*When I take the time to think about you, I can't regret one bit that you were my boo.*

*The things we did were so pure, I honestly don't think there's a cure.*

*I don't think I've ever loved so strongly.*

*There is no explanation why you were so dear.*

*Crystals were no comparison to how our love was so clear.*

*Everything was so rightly done, never misunderstanding.*

*Words could never explain how freely my heart soared.*

*The way I feel, it seems like I was lured.*

*So unreal!*

*No doubt in my mind that you were adored.*

*Would I do it all over again?—yeah sure!*

*Times were hard, yet not once did I deny it.*

*When I was with you, I felt so at home.*

*If we joined the halves of our hearts, they would fit.*

*Because I could feel your heart speak to mine.*

*Your touch made my heart foam.*

*You made my love so real.*

*Like a star shining far in the sky,*

*That's how you made me feel.*

*I can't possibly say good-bye.*

*Because our love is just so real.*

## SLEEPING WHISPERS

*He's asleep now, tightly curled into a position of quiet comfort.*

*No sounds are heard, and no words being uttered, only colorless images inside his frontal lobe.*

*I'm watching...watching his blissfulness and the way his body lays there motionless.*

*His face displays no emotion, which only makes me wonder more, what's behind his closed eyes.*

*I want to whisper into his ear things that only my subconscious knows how to say.*

*If I could persuade him to believe there should be no more delay, then maybe, maybe he would perceive that this is more than just a phase, you see.*

*There are many ways to love. Some love with passion and some with commitment, but I, I assure you my love is not intermittent.*

*See, I've tried to throw this away as just another day—I'm just another victim of his game that he tries to rename and claim that me and all the other girls are all the same.*

*If I could just whisper into his ear and relay all the things I want him to hear.*

*I would begin to say—my love for you goes beyond any emotion to describe, or a feeling you wish could come again by making amends.*

*I love you more than just with my heart or my mind, I love you with my soul, and that my friend—is more than you'll ever know.*

*'Cause I'm sitting here, admiring you from your head to the tip of your toe, telling myself...*

*If I could just whisper into his ear, all the things I want him to hear.*

## SO I SAID GOODBYE

*I was fed up. I was tired of living a lie. I knew he wasn't for me.*

*He had done nothing but taken from me.*

*Not material things...but*

*My goals were delayed—my determination was deterred—my dedication was declined*

*...and admitting my responsibility—I denied.*

*A complete waste of my time, no peace of mind...Somebody say— but God!*

*He opened my eyes so that I had cried my last cry!*

*A year gone by and I was finally able to wave goodbye.*

*Warning to my ladies...those of us who say we want a good man, Don't be fooled. I'm not try'na be rude.*

*But please believe...guys are experts at setting the right mood.*

*Sex does not mean he loves you.*

*I know we like to fantasize that if we take it up a notch, he'll fall in love.*

*Let me be the one to say.*

*When a man sleeps with a woman that he does not love...or even care about,*

*He's only getting his itch scratched.*

*And ladies, open legs are nothing but hydrocortisone, and now his itch is gone.*

*So, I've learned how important it is for me to wait!*

*It's just a shame that it took this long for me to get it straight, but it's never too late!*

*Y'all, I had simply become his habit, and whatever he needed; he thought he could have it.*

*And like Keanu in 'The Matrix'—I must have swallowed the wrong tablet, 'cause he was fast.*

*Fast like a rabbit, and I looked right pass it—his skills were fantastic.*

*Disgust in my stomach, excuse me so I can spit—it's time to jump over this shhhh.*

*Yeah, he wasn't a good fit.*

*Hands to my face in disbelief; I never knew this relief would be so sweet.*

*Opposite is my expression, not hello or hi, he was not the right guy.*

*You just witnessed my process of waving goodbye.*

# VOLUME 5

Giving up on life entered my mind more and more in those passing days. I would even check out of school early and go home just to cry. I wasn't sure I knew life without my knight. From my limited perspective, he was my life. As badly as I wanted to hate him, I couldn't. I was so lost—each day just kind of, went by. My ambitious drive was diminishing, and my goals and values were a blurry sight. I had about an ounce of hope left—so I held on tight. I told myself, "God is gonna take me so far away from this hurt, this pain, and all the people who caused it. I'm going to rid everyone of Erinn since she's not good enough for any of you." That thought alone made me wish for it even harder.

I desired so much more out of life, but I had been drained—emptied out. I loved my knight, I loved my mom, and I loved my dad. Problem was I felt like Mom didn't know me, and I was still getting to know this man imposing as my dad. Sometimes, I wished that he had never gone to rehab. I was so mad and angry at the world and at myself. This boy had caused me to lose so much of all the me I had left. I did things just to get back at him, make him hurt like I hurt, but all I did was devalue myself more and more. He wasn't looking. I wasn't important. It just wasn't fair!

After graduation, that summer floated on by. We were cordial to one another, my knight and I, though it didn't mean I wasn't still in love with him. Pause for a strong memory. Still can't tell you why he did it, but it mattered that he did. Graduation party, limited guest list, I'm on it.  I go, why not, he's still my boo—to me.  There's a weird energy, but a soothing comfort of being known by the family.  I was the friend, the one always around, the girl next door, the one he studied with, the one allowed over when mom was home, invited to the BBQ—I been here, this mine! I absorbed that comfort to help me get through the awkward glances and child-like interactions. Teens! I mean, my knight was still my knight from my point of view.  Even if he wasn't.  Fast forward, the party ends, and he's counting his coins from all the cards.  Take this in with me, ok.  He sends for me.  Yeah, you heard me, "go get Erinn, I need her," is what he said y'all! Hesitantly, I walk in, "yes?" "Here, hold this please," he instructs. I start holding the money as I'm instructed. Only me—just me. I hold all the money he counts.  He hands it directly to me. The others in the room just sit in silence as they witness what none of us fully understand. I say nothing, I look down, I smile towards my chest…only for me. Get this…the 'actual' girlfriend was present…right there in the very same room., inches from me. No lie! I think to myself, "this is trust, this is his heart, these are the words unspoken, it was real."   We catch a glance into one another's eyes—just a glance, but it was intimate, it was vivid, it was enough. Nothing more was needed.

## RHYTHM

*Oooh ah, oooh ah, oooh ah,*

*I'm doing it, doing it, I'm doing it,*

*Feeling it, feeling it, I'm feeling it,*

*I'm moving it, I'm moving it, moving it,*

*Go with me, flow with me.*

*Perfect tracing of my curves as they explode colorfully into your soul.*

*Work it, work it—do what you gotta do in order to achieve the chance to go higher.*

*These tunes carry a burning desire,*

*For my body to invade your shyness and cause an eruption of fire.*

*I know you sense the intensity because this beat that we're moving to is more than what it seems, you see…*

*I don't want to push, but this is 3$^{rd}$ grade skill.*

*And I need you to know that your entire being has my sweat glands leaking.*

*Shade your eyes, cover me, I'm an eclipse; Swollen lips accentuated, dame un beso, gimmie kiss.*

*From boys to men, grown men, this water's deep…the waves are growing.*

*It seems now a days that there's something wrong with a woman wanting what she wants…how and when she wants it—unlike ya average girl.*

*These pulsing sounds are dictating the rolling of my hips.*

*And have taken over the feeling all the way to my fingertips.*

*Anticipate the vibrations as they flow from the bottom my ground dwellers,*

*And move to the top of my thoughts.*

*If I could compare, my rhythm would be wind with its highs and lows, cools and hots—I just got to get you into me.*

*I hear the beats climbing and climbing, reaching ultimate pleasure.*

*Hold on now—you bet not stop cause I'm dancing at the top.*

*That's my spot…don't stop, don't stop, don't stop.*

*You feel my rhythm?!*

## AND SUDDENLY

*I thought it was true—I thought I knew you.*

*Intense coals of fire burning into my soul.*

*Prickling of my flesh—why am I so blue?*

*A woman of grace bright in smile.*

*I held my rod for a while.*

*Love should not capture me again.*

*For being hurt is just not my style.*

*If I want you gone—why does my heart still long?*

*To be held by your tender embrace,*

*While listening to our favorite song.*

*The memories continue to sing.*

*One night, one look, one touch, one kiss—oh, how I do miss.*

*The rain and the tears streaming down your chin.*

*As I laid in your arms, girlfriend, boyfriend…the end.*

*Damn, I must be blind.*

*I knew you weren't mine.*

*But wise words have been quoted.*

*Headline…never say never.*

*'Cause as you can see,*

*You're no longer worth my timeline.*

# *ABOVE THE CHALLENGE*

*I am above the challenge!*

*My head is high—and that it shall remain.*

*When I am down, I shall not sigh.*

*For I know—I shall rise!*

*And yes, I rise—I rise—I rise!*

*And yes, I rise!*

## FOGET ME NOTS

Lost inside a deep, dark hole; lost is the love that filled my soul.

Blinded is my heart; blinded right from the start.

All the way to the top, does the water cover me,

Until no more the light I can see.

Sequestered from my only knowing; forever will my tears keep flowing.

Now, just when roses turned red,

And violets were finally blue,

While my love for you was being declared,

That's when you left me with no clue.

Yes, birds still fly, and water is still wet.

In the sunlight, the flower still will bloom.

Just as naturally as these do exist,

So is my love for you in the midst.

Of trouble, of joy, of pain,

There's no one left but me to blame.

For you, I endured midnight's hour.

For you, I'd climb the highest tower.

Forever will your love be written on my heart.

Forever will I feel the feeling of your touch.

Forever when the stars are high in the sky.

Forever will I smile of you and I.

## THE SONG IN MY SOUL

*I put my soul in these words; unspoken passion in each verb.*

*To the closed mind, may sound a bit absurd.*

*Relax ya mind, take time to hear my rhyme—what you said—ya heard!*

*At times, my written words are an unknown language that will send your thoughts into deep mental anguish.*

*I'm only trying to relay my message.*

*Do you know now why the caged bird sings?*

*If you're locked away with no control of your captivity, learn to embrace your spirituality.*

*I may be wrong in my interpretation, you see, but Patrick Henry said, "Give me death or give me liberty."*

*And to me, freedom is more than a state to be; it's a mentality.*

*A mentality that's been cultivated to rise—above any obstacle, any limitation,*

*And every label that has named you less than who you are.*

*And to their surprise, more than the right to go left if you'd like and the privilege to go right if you choose.*

*No more will mental slavery destroy and confuse.*

*The power to rise…rise above it all—is in us.*

*The caged bird sings not for you to hear; you simply reaped the enjoyment.*

*He is singing, he is peaceful, he is steady.*

*From observation with your eyes, you see—his soul has been set free*

## BITTERSWEET

*When I first met you, my eyes were shut.*

*Over the years, I had placed a shield there…as my defense.*

*And suddenly, I was trapped by this emotion. My once simple life now made no sense.*

*Because, before I was aware, I had slipped you my heart.*

*And that was not what I had planned.*

*I wanted to take things slow, you know, let it flow.*

*But to my surprise, I have taken a dive, headfirst,*

*Only to be left in a very familiar place.*

*Hurt, betrayal, regret, which one do I embrace?*

*Blaming you is not my goal, but rather to gain back my self-control.*

*I have learned that love is always a possibility.*

*Even when I thought, for me, it wasn't meant to be.*

*I believe with all my soul—if it's really me, that your arms want to hold, your actions will begin to show.*

*You know how I feel; you know it's real.*

*It's your choice from here.*

*As I write, my eyes begin to tear.*

*But whatever your decision about me and you,*

*Thank you for this priceless rendezvous!*

## *TIME*

*Time, where did you go?*
*You were just by my side.*
*I never realized I was in for a ride.*
*Because you left without even saying goodbye.*

*Time, we've had some good moments.*
*I love how you give me an extra hour,*
*But then turn and take it away.*
*Don't we all wish you could stay?*

*From young to old, we all know.*
*One day time will show,*
*Whether we sank or swam.*
*Through all the trials, frown or smile.*

*Along the path, I found a better friend.*
*Time, this friend won't leave me.*
*Sweet are the memories that stay 'til the end.*
*While time flies, memories stand by.*

## DUST THE WEBS

*Somebody, please confiscate these tears; every attempt, all that shows are my fears.*

*My thoughts are terribly bent,*

*Opening up all over again.*

*This is harder than trusting the weather—I sit, and I contemplate on where to begin.*

*And all I do is wonder; will we ever be together?*

*Does the sign on my back read "NO GOOD?"*

*By their side is where I always stood.*

*This is my earnest plea; comprehending this madness is like insanity.*

*It always feels like the right one. Will I ever be capable of exhaling? When does my true love come? Because I'm so disgusted with this trite failing.*

*I never say what I really feel...And before I know it, they're gone away. Then the depression makes my heart want to spill.*

*Lost inside myself, that's where I stay.*

*Games, deception, and unmade endless promises, but it was never that serious.*

*Then my heart confesses...girl, he was only being curious.*

*Feels like I've lost all hope, yet I must carry on.*

*I've got to be strong; one day that real love will come along.*

*So I dust the webs away. My real man will come.*

*I believe he will stay.*

*And he'll understand just where I'm coming from.*

## THOUGHTS

*It was a cold night, and I was thinking about you.*

*I never thought a light could shine so true.*

*At night, I wonder if it's a dream,*

*Because I've never felt so warm, it seems.*

*When I hear a soft sound,*

*All I want is for you to be around.*

*Your love is like rain,*

*Falling down, erasing all the pain.*

*The way I feel when we're together,*

*I ask, will I feel this free forever?*

*When you look at me,*

*I know we were meant to be.*

## CONFUSION

*My heart is in a puddle of despair,*

*I thought you would love me too.*

*While all the time that I was loving you,*

*Never were you there.*

*Confusion has entered my soul,*

*I'm walking alone on this path.*

*My eyes show nothing but the wrath,*

*For all the deceit that was untold.*

*All my opportunities and chances you threw away.*

*Regret lives in my mind, day and night.*

*Memories made this love feel so right.*

*But it's got me thinking, should I go or stay?*

*Confusion startles my sleep.*

*Dreariness lurks in my thoughts.*

*Forever, my heart will you keep.*

*But I know the war could've at least been fought.*

*Light blue skies remind me of your smile,*

*It will never leave my sight.*

*Confusion only makes it a longer mile.*

*Make me stop and tell me it'll be alright.*

## TEARS

*Don't take my tears for weakness.*

*They symbolize the endurance of my ancestors.*

*They coincide with the tears of the Son.*

*Don't take my tears for weakness.*

*It seemed harder to let them fall, than to not.*

*In each drop of tear, I am letting go.*

*I am closing another door that need not stay open.*

*Away from hindrances, I am walking.*

*I am taking back the authority my Father gave me.*

*And you sit there with your head shaking,*

*Not understanding my cry—here's why.*

*There is power in my tears because they wash me.*

*They keep me in remembrance of what He did for me on Calvary!*

*Reminding me there is no reason to go back,*

*And every reason to press forward.*

*So, when you see me all wet-faced and crying rivers,*

*When you see currents of tears streaming from my eyes,*

*When you see waterfalls pouring down my cheek,*

*Know, that my tears will forever,*

*Victoriously fall!*

# VOLUME 6

We went our separate ways to college and a life unknown to either of us. I was so ready for something out of the ordinary...something exciting. Immediately, the depression lifted. Those first couple of weeks, I did whatever would make *me* feel good. No more weight or pressure from this person or that person. My shoulders were light as feathers. I drifted into the fearless wave of no care in the world. I was fierce in a way that I dared someone to cross me. "I'm in charge now," I told myself.

There it was—college—a plethora of new faces to see and interesting people to meet, so much in my arm's reach. I must try this—oh, and that! Dialogues I never thought I would have. Experiences no one will ever nor should know I had. Oh me, oh my! I was having the time of my life, and for the first time, a boy was not the center of my universe—I was. I needed rest from the daggers that had stabbed me in my back, rest from the daggers I had placed in backs, rest from the ditches I dug and the lies I not only told others—but even the ones I made myself believe, and rest from the constant agony of sleepless nights with sad love songs pressed against my ears. There was very little trust left in me for men or females, and I wasn't interested in anyone trying to change that. From what I've shared so far, notice I didn't have many friends. Most of them were exposed for who they really were—they were disloyal and had stabbed me in the back and had the audacity to stick around until I had realized it. I didn't trust many people at all. The few friends I had were family, mostly cousins, and to this day I'm so thankful for their part in my life. If not for them, the few, I wouldn't even believe in the possibility of safe friendships or loyalty. Shout out to my day one bestie and my cousin besties! And those I've gained as besties along the way! Love y'all!

I remember that first Christmas break when I went home. There was this familiar stench in the atmosphere. I knew that feeling oh too well. I did my best to enjoy the short visit and make the best of it. Finally, it was time to see you know who. I hadn't forgotten what pain he had caused me, yet still, there I was, nervous…the last memory of him hung in my mind like a wall portrait in an art gallery—it was ugly, but I was still eager to be lost in my delayed fantasy. He still wanted me. He still thought of me. He missed me just like I missed him. Was this the real thing? What would it be like? Would it be like it used to be? Before it was broken? There he was—my knight. His armor, however, was not so shiny anymore. We talked about how college life was and how we had missed each other. It was weird because there was this unspoken knowledge that our vibe was not the same. I played it off like I didn't notice. We laughed and he held me. As my mind drifted, I was flooded with many different emotions and realities. I saw myself throughout the years. I'd lost friends, hope, and even a part of myself to the likes of this boy. I admitted to myself that I had subconsciously defined Erinn through him. I didn't like the truth of that confrontation. I decided I wanted to change the scene and get a new script. As I returned to the present moment, I remember looking at him and feeling the fear lodged in the back of my throat because I knew this was the end. We repeated the motions over and over. I suppose we were both anticipating with hope the familiar feelings to return as they once had. For me, they never came. It was such a foreign emotion I didn't even know if I should be disappointed or happy. I didn't know when, and wasn't even aware of it until that moment, but I was not in love with this boy anymore. Wow!

## *I LET IT OUT*

*So, I can't explain the whirlwind of my heart; can't undo the gash the pain left behind, so the sun can't shine. Broken promises, broken hearts carrying all the pieces—this is a long path to travel—the path we journeyed though; when did it crumble?*

*Haters—they'd marvel at the rarity of our union because the language of our souls caused a transfusion, but I'm trying to rid myself of this memory, the imprint you abandoned, the song in my head, the touch beneath my skin—it lingers like a loud aroma on Sunday morning after the rain stops pouring.*

*I can still taste you—your facial indentations are painted in my frontal lobe, beginning to robe my mouth with your lips against this pleasure & bliss. This—fight seems never-ending. I'm searching night and day for the answers—somebody, please, tell me how to walk away from this…Tell me; how when you love so strongly; can the recipient stay blinded to your affection, a completely deaf ear to your screaming passion?*

*How you would do anything, be anything, yet simultaneously…you need to disappear from my sight, leave my name out of your mouth, don't speak of us—leave us in that night. The atmosphere no longer needs to hear—how you were absent from me—standing adjacent yet completely complacent, not knowing how bent my emotions had been from withdrawal—you, who has not looked back to say sorry who strides away in a hurry—no mind to my feelings; you, who believes I did nothing to convince of my loyalty*

*As if for me, this walk has been just a cup a sweet tea.*

*Who told the world I was your own & always would be?*

*You have become like a vapor, who when my eyes have reopened, I will see what I missed at first glance 'cause you never gave me the chance—you showered with attention, ecstasy, and the actions to follow. I understand why you would wait to introduce us—to capture my trust. So unfair to think I wouldn't care. Of course I do, that's why I feel so betrayed. You waited and lured me until my love was pending into the deep, then you martyred my soul for believing in you—is that what they mean by code blue?*

*You were never really there, not the 'you' I loved, somehow, you left me standing at the alter with anticipation. Rising with the beat of every word, you spun me into a web of lies, rapping my lyrics and soothing all my cries...you were an imposter, my heart, stolen from the roster. A list I should have remained on until you had been long gone.*

*Good-bye to the man you imposed as, the man who ran away and left me in his past.*

*Good-bye to the tears I've shed, the prayers I have led, the lonely nights I left splattered on our bed. I look at you and I see a black out—I blacked out, not aware of the unconscious desire to be loved & wanted by you. You have to go, outside, away from my heart— I don't know where, but here's a good start—tarry pass the fence and onto the street's pavements—mark my words, get out, I let it out...I let this out, yet still, it remains within! Glued to my skin, cuddled up like a bear rug against my skin. Covers pulled back, settled in to reside—I thought I said good-bye!*

*Compromise got my spirit man tongue-tied—stayed too long, and now my soul tied.*

*I can't explain the whirlwind of my heart—I can't undo the gash the pain left behind, so the sun can't shine—so I confess dysfunction in the spirit of my mind.*

*Broken up, rolled up, and puffed like a blunt. The world has abused my use, and I—like others became a living noose—hanging my value with constant excuse—says the lie that came just to reduce it. Leaving character behind—assassinated—dead to the truth, rendered blind—so you see, I have to say good-bye, because staying says I'm ready to die.*

## HOME

*I know it's not any good for me, yet still, there's something on the inside of me that just won't let go of Pontiac.*

*B.K.A. Yaktown, it's my hometown.*

*It's like this pipe that's calling my name, and I'm twisted up in this game.*

*It represents everything that I don't want, so tell me, why my mind is so distraught?*

*It's like I'm fiending for that next hit, asking myself, is this really all my fault?*

*I keep longing for the first high because I don't really know how to say goodbye. One part of me is far away in the place that I should be, while the other part is screaming—I just want to be free from the ball and chain, to be me, immediately. I feel like a stranger in my own house, there's no intimacy.*

*This is backwards though.*

*I'm supposed to be writing about love, peace, and happiness, but lately, my words lack the finesse. I fell on my knees—I beg the Lord, please...*

*I think these birds have built a nest—I feel it in my chest, I must confess.*

*There was a Boone in my left, while the Black was in my right.*

*EB, that's what they call me, but who is she?*

*I'm searching...searching, looking, seeking so desperately to find the time to just devote to my mind—the thoughts just circle around.*

*Am I supposed to be here, or am I simply running out of fear?*

*I don't get any sleep, my nights are long...thinking about everything that has gone wrong.*

*How did I end up all alone—this was supposed to be home.*

*I've been standing in this maze for so many days, seeking for strategic ways,*

*To find my way back home.*

*That's where my heart really belongs.*

## CRY ANYWAY

*Sometimes, you just gotta let the tears fall,*

*Even when you don't know where they're coming from,*

*Or why they're falling.*

*Sometimes, you just gotta cry it out,*

*For the times you brushed off how you felt,*

*Or didn't realize how you felt,*

*Or outright didn't acknowledge how you felt.*

*Sometimes, you just gotta let the tears fall,*

*To allow yourself to feel the humanity of it all,*

*To confront the fact that somebody did drop you, abandon you, lie to you, lie on you, betray you, steal from you, cheat on you...they did.*

*And because you refused to be a victim, you ran.*

*Not knowing you caused more damage by not healing first.*

*So cry—cry today, tomorrow, cry this very second if need be.*

*Feel what it feels like to feel.*

*Become aware of that emotion.*

*Nurture it—don't neglect it.*

*Sometimes, you just gotta let the tears fall.*

*I do—I just did.*

*And from it, came this—so you see, let them fall.*

*They won't hinder your greatness.*

## GENERATIONAL CURSE

*An ignorant people, supposedly educated, but ignorant people.*

*Why do our children not know what these stones mean?*

*Maybe because we have forgotten what was once known.*

*Disruptions in the pit of my stomach because my taste buds reject sweet mixed with sour.*

*If only we knew what was in our power; what mountains we were meant to conquer and devour, instead of backing down like cowards.*

*Saul, He said—Kill these people, saving none.*

*Yet, just as we do—he must keep some.*

*See, Lord—for You, this I do…*

*And God's response…depart from me, you worker of iniquity, you I never knew.*

*Generational, conspiring, and intentional deceit.*

*Lies that have been told over and over, and over—it's ourselves that we defeat.*

*No longer is there a covering, no longer do we protect, respect, or positively affect.*

*That's why we have Generation X and ecstasy in our school system because it is the fantasy of the flesh that's being fulfilled instead of obedience to the Master's will.*

*Immorality has become an epidemic—our nation, as it stands is internally sick.*

*And with each other are we in conflict—not recognizing the snare of the enemy created to constrict.*

*But he can only constrain that which you have allowed him to contain.*

*Our land, our homes, our families, our children.*

*We can't breathe, and how is it no one has noticed we've turned pale with blue lips from suffocation—and it was God who said His people perish for lack of knowledge.*

*We do not know Him.*

*With churches and educational establishments, with a rich history of people whose lives were taken—and given for our sake—for the opportunity of freedom from mental and physical captivity, illiteracy, inequality, and most importantly...*

*There is never any substitute for integrity.*

*I write with anger—I write with rage—I write with a heart that cries for such a blind age.*

*Infected with disease, loving the ways of our enemies.*

*Right now...we see in part, we know in part, but when we see Him—do we even desire to be like Him?*

*We laugh at the 2-year-old that uses profanity, saying, look, she's a mini me.*

*Not knowing we're demonstrating insanity.*

*What's the definition of the person we seek to be?*

*Doing the same thing again and again—expecting different results.*

*A generational curse—see Momma did it, you did it, and now baby girl will do it too.*

*Do as I say, not as I do—but what you do, is all I see.*

*The weak mind of just enough is what cripples our potential.*

*It's like having wings, but never trying to fly; a voice, but never lifting it to be heard.*

*We settle for the table's crumbs, all the while complaining because our change never did come.*

*Our children are crying.*

*Will it end with you so it can begin with me?*

*Will you teach me my name—one that I can read and write?*

*Will you show me right from wrong according to the Word?*

*Is it ok if I speak correct grammar and not be ashamed?*

*Because it's not called sounding white…*

*But rather knowing that I too am intellectually, bright.*

*Will you raise me to know I am a child of the Most High?*

*So that when this world attacks, I know whose got my back.*

*Rules are ok—love knowledge, and discipline too.*

*It's really up to you.*

*So what's it going to be—Mom, Dad…Church?*

*Will you give me hope—Will I be born into the curse?*

*Or will you be the one to break it first?*

*Will you—will you—will you?*

*Will you break this generational curse?*

## LOVE IN MOTION

*Love can be as sweet as the sound of a bird going tweet.*

*The sincerity of a virgin heart could take eons to break apart.*

*Love doesn't cause or bring hate—if so, it wasn't love, just dead weight.*

*True love will never vex or tire—and the motion will never expire.*

*The blooming of a lily,*

*The rushing, mighty roar of the ocean,*

*So intense, yet none can compare,*

*To the love that we share.*

*Will the fire last, or will it fade into our past?*

*The twinkle in your eye is my eternal light—a warm and breezy night.*

*With stars in the sky—out hearts will yet fly.*

*Whisper into my ear the sweet sound of love I want to hear.*

*The mutual feeling, coming from above—will soar, forever within, like a dove.*

*The blooming of a lily,*

*The rushing, mighty roar of the ocean,*

*So intense, yet none can compare,*

*To the love that we share.*

## SPRING

*Spring, came that year, bitter sweet. Hindsight is what they call the best sight. And yeah, sure, looking back allows you to remember where you were, forces you to acknowledge what you didn't know.*

*My mind was fresh, ready to embark upon what I thought was the start of my red-carpet runway. You know how you walk with your head held high, feet falling in the perfect stride...proudly prancing through the lilies, looking like, they ain't got nothing on me. Smack dab in the heart of my hopes, I was gutted of all my desires—laying against the ropes, open and exposed, vulnerable to the harsh rain's pour.*

*I realized there was no cover, no shade tree to hover or block me from the vindictive elements. So, I put on the face, played the part people wanna see.*

*I looked resilient, I looked victorious, but I didn't believe my own facade.*

*Truth was, I was crushed to the marrow of my bones, broken pass the point of putting the pieces back together. Everything in me wanted to crawl into that dark hole that called my name on those lonely nights, but someday, someway, somehow, somewhere, somebody kept me, pushed me, held me, and consoled me...comforted me in a matter that passed even my own understanding.*

*See, people needed to know, wanted to know, thought they knew but didn't have a clue.*

*I can't tell you how, I can only tell you Who. So I was consoled, all the while unfolding the treasure this vessel had been holding...I'm beholding my face in the mirror as He does the molding. And though it was a little touch and go there for a minute, let me testify, see, I had to fake it to make it. I had to not feel because the alternative was my mind...he comes to steal and kill—and though I didn't see my joy being ripped apart and my confidence being eaten on by sadness, I could smell her...the stench of the soul rotting, dying, his task is to destroy.*

*Yet in His Sovereignty, the Master that is, He mapped out each step, saw each footprint, spoke into each path—detailing my destiny.*

*Y'all might laugh, only because you don't understand if it were up to my grasp, I would've let go...*

*My prayers were so bleak, I didn't even know what to ask, hurt making me focus on my past, y'all I'm telling you I wasn't gonna last, but life is full of hello and good-byes, so I had to take off that mask and wave farewell to that old man and his lies.*

*I've made it through some tough rains that often made it hard not to complain. Along the way, I've gained some growing pains, learned how to call on Jesus name.*

*After these showers, there will be harvest, there will be fruit, there will be gladness—I aint' accepting anything less, that's just madness.*

*On us all, a little rain must fall, don't give up before you witness the flowers... then is the sun at its brightest! He'll never leave you, especially in the darkest hour.*

## LOVE BEING LOVE

*Love being love, it could never betray. So, is it fair to say I fooled myself?*

*Love being love, it would never walk away. So, is it fair to say I left way too soon?*

*Back n Forth n Back—I go...fighting to convince myself to leave, to go, to depart.*

*Ripping my eardrums with the volume of my thoughts...I can't hear my sanity anymore.*

*All I hear are songs of us, all I feel are breath-taking moments we left in the dust.*

*One attempt after another, reneging on my truth—I'm still in love with you! So what am I supposed to do?*

*Love being love, it forgives every wrong. So, is it fair to say I have truly forgiven?*

*Love being love, it bears all things. So, is it fair to say I gave up on us?*

*Back n Forth n Back—I go...competing with myself to see how long before the next daydream. Determined to keep going, not stopping, fast forward...to the best chapters of my life. My mind pleads with me to get a grip on this, while my heart forever remembers the passion and power of that first kiss. Our souls manufactured, one for the other—I'm in the garden where we met. I don't understand why you have not come for me yet.*

*Love being love, its patience is everlasting. So, is it fair to say I should just wait?*

*Love being love, it always hopes. So, is it fair to say I have not lost my hope?*

*Back n Forth n Back—I go...*

## BLACK BEAUTY

*Sweet Dark Mahogany, I am thinking of me—sitting under the beginning of the setting sun—light that reminds me, I am someone.*

*Clothed in arabian silk, while my skin glistens.*

*Sweet Dark Mahogany, I am thinking of me—with the softness of my lips as they compliment every dip in my hips.*

*Why? Well, I think it's the creativity of my Maker. I'm the flavor in your salt shaker.*

*The melanin in my skin has given me a color of quiet toffee.*

*Don't you enjoy the way the Son has passionately blessed me?*

*Sweet Dark Mahogany, I am thinking of me—and the way I see you in me.*

*When you smile, I see a reflection of pearls, and when you move, the atmosphere is flattered.*

*Don't listen to the negative vibes, they're just jealous of our natural high.*

*Sweet Dark Mahogany, I am thinking of me—I see me in your curls, A.K.A. kinks—and I know how to appreciate the ash right after a shower.*

*Because only then can the lotion be rubbed on with sentiment and romantic power.*

*My sweet dark mahogany, don't let anyone call you anything differently.*

*Be who you are—*

*Our Maker's joy, His workmanship, the apple of His eye, shining like a star.*

*Sweet darkness, you are the compilation and completion of a*
*rainbow,*
*the origination of what we know.*
*Sweet Dark Mahogany, I am thinking of me—and how all colors*
*belong to thee,*
*And beautiful is what I see.*
*You are truly Sweet Dark Mahogany—thinking of me.*

## MUCH BETTER THAN THAT

*Fall, Winter, Spring, and Summer,*

*Showers, flowers, colors, and beauty,*

*So much delight in that little cutie,*

*Nope, much better than that.*

*Ice cream—extra large sundae with nuts.*

*Sipping lemonade in the scorching sun.*

*And all the fun of Summer life has just begun.*

*Still, I tell you, You ain't seen nothing yet.*

*I'm talking 'bout peace, love, and joy.*

*Goodness and mercy just to name a few.*

*A way is made—doors are opened.*

*Comfortless will I never be—maaaan, you ain't got a clue.*

*Jesus—yeah, that's Who He is!*

*Walks with me and He talks with me.*

*He gives me authority over the enemy.*

*Oh, and did you know, He's given me a sound mind.*

*I have life and that more abundantly.*

*Forget a temporary feel good.*

*Blessings galore has He bestowed.*

*And even paid, the debt that I owed.*

*This world and its false visions,*

*Will never compare.*

*It only ends in depair.*

*But Jesus—I know…beyond the facts,*

*Is so much better than that!*

# *TODAY*

*Like brand new mercies each day,*

*Like freshly bloomed lilies on a new spring day,*

*Like the morning's dew from the moisture of the night,*

*Today, I love you.*

*More than yesterday and eager for tomorrow,*

*Stronger than when we first met,*

*Today, I love you.*

*With refreshed, brand-new love,*

*Today, I fell in love with you,*

*All over, and forever, again.*

# VOLUME 7

Being over him didn't come with a step-by-step recipe on how to stop missing him. I never calculated how hard it would be to make my actions catch up to what my heart had already realized. I had no idea—no idea of the residue I still had to deal with and how this heartbreak had become a trauma I'd come face to face with again. I was, however, determined to move on. It was clear to me that he didn't want me, but I had to receive that truth internally for myself. I had lied to myself for so long that the truth was no easy pill to swallow. Life and living it each day was a glass of water helping me to swallow the pills as I learned from trials and lessons alike. In college, oh, I learned a lot honey, and not just from my studies. Boys in college thought they were so smart, so smooth. Their sweet words and endearing comments; it was the laughter of my day. Little did they know I had already had some crash course lesson on boys—my eyes were a bit wider. I was that much privier to the game. Didn't like the pain, but I'm forever grateful for the experience. College was also exposing me to things outside my little box. Experiences that caused me to learn just how quickly one mistake could impact you for the rest of your life. As painful as it was to let go, I knew holding on to him was not going to benefit me at all.

My thinking was maturing, believe it or not. I was growing up! Yes—hurt, broken, confused, mad at the world, Erinn, was growing!!! The process was oh so necessary! I remembered my past heartache, and I vowed to myself that I wouldn't allow someone to take me like that again. Oh yes, the walls went up! I wanted to love again, but I didn't want to lose who I was as a result. Character change doesn't happen over night. I learned from that relationship what to look out for, but I still had a way to go. I desired to be better though. I convinced myself that when I went home for the summer, I would be a better person. I would be a better daughter to my parents. I began owning some of the responsibility for my own life and the decisions I made. God really broke open the revelation to me that my actions and my behaviors were a choice, and that blame was no longer on anyone else. People are responsible for how they handle you, but you are responsible for what you do about it. I was not making responsible decisions, and Erinn, and only Erinn, could change that. I started thinking about my parents and what it was like for them to have had to deal with me. I wondered what their thoughts about me were. Did they only see the behavior, or did they see pass it to me? I wanted them to see me in a better light. I wanted them to know I could be better. Listen, when God reveals our ugliness to us—it is not a good feeling. Not at all.

If I wanted it badly enough—it should just happen, right? How differently that summer played out than what I was thinking in my mind. I suppose for my *own* attempt, I did fairly well for about two weeks. TWO WEEKS PEOPLE!! It wasn't long before I jumped back into the comfort of the fast lane. The late-night parties, the drugs, the drinking, this guy, that guy—this had become my thing. It was more in control of me than I was of it.

Simply wanting it to stop wasn't enough. I needed help! This was my pattern. Can we really admit how hard it is to break or unlearn the patterns, good or bad, we've always known? From the outside view, I looked a mess, and I was, but I was also bleeding— mentally, spiritually, and emotionally. I had no clue what to do about it or how to care for my invisible wounds. That summer took me to a very low point in my life and I was once again, disfigured with confusion. By now, my best friend had come home from college. Our bond was still just as strong, and it got much stronger that summer. Everything I enjoyed that summer was in the total opposite direction of becoming a better person. It didn't stop God's plan though…those maturing thoughts that I was having—it was God doing that. God won't write you off like people do at times. He never let me go. That summer, of 2002, something happened in me, and I haven't been the same since. My taste buds changed, physically and spiritually. I had a real encounter with God. He spoke to me; I thought I was hearing things, but it was time. His timing! A real change had been set in motion. He was using it all for my good.

When I returned to school, I had to fight internal battles every day. I had no idea what was causing my thinking to be so different. Even my friends didn't understand why I didn't want to go to parties or drink with them anymore. Shoot, I didn't even have a precise or clear explanation myself. Not yet, at least, but I knew I liked it. This is what I wanted. God had been listening to my prayers. He had heard me all those nights I had cried out for help. I knew there was more to life than what I'd seen. I knew I had to change, but it wasn't possible on my own. Thank God for hearing me! He hadn't forgotten about me after all. Just know, this was a process. Nothing sustainable happened overnight. I had to learn to walk in and apply the principles—and the truths that God was revealing to me. That wasn't easy. I mean, I'm in college, folks. There's a lot going on around me that makes it easy to slip, to slide, and best believe I was going to be tried. What I do miss most about those days though, was the time spent with my girls. We would all gather in each other's rooms and watch movies, or have confession night, create college dorm meals, or just pamper one another. Just talking life out together. Sisterhood is a powerful thing. Priceless were the moments we shared, the tears we cried together, the laughs, the jokes, the pranks—oh, the pranks! Why do I have this vivid memory of this game we had going on with several people on campus involved? It was called "tighten up." Y'all, we were young and dumb, as the saying goes. Tighten up consisted of catching a person completely off guard and slapping them on their butt as hard as you could while yelling Tighten Up! Then you ran away so they couldn't get to you for retaliation. Oh, buddy—if you got someone just right…your angle was good, your ambush was precise…you could really make some enemies from that slap. LOL! Still makes me laugh to this day. These were the moments, though. Memories were made, and relationships formed that would go on to last forever.

## NO OTHER LOVE

*Sweeter than the honeycomb's honey, softer than the silk known as Egyptian,*

*Still water with dew-filled melodies, passionately, promising purpose,*

*Having already paid the price—for my soul, Lord, how much did it cost?*

*See, I was lost without a trace.*

*Looking in the mirror, I couldn't recognize even my own face.*

*But God's grace—He took my place!*

*He boldly broke barriers, becoming the very stone the builders rejected.*

*The shining star that dark night—the slain Lamb—the Great I Am!*

*It's not until you've had the imitation that you know…*

*There's no other love.*

*Not until you've seen loneliness face to face, not until giving up is your only hope.*

*It's only then that you know…*

*There's no other love.*

*It's not until your lowest point has been reached—your mind can't find peace.*

*And your soul has fainted that you know…*

*There's no other love.*

*Breath-giving, peace-dispensing, hope-fulfilling love.*

*Without hesitation—humbling Himself.*

*Lion of Judah, Holy God!*

*There's no other love.*

*Surely, saving souls—dying, even though repulsed by His own—*

*The mystery... if only they had known.*

*By His Spirit, revelations unfold, so His story has been told!*

*Now you know...*

*There's no other love.*

## THE PRESENCE OF GOD

*Have you ever felt that feeling of an unknown presence hanging around you at times?*

*Have you ever been alone and it seems as though you're not?*

*Then there are those times when you may actually hear a voice.*

*And it's not just in your mind; You really do hear the voice echoing inside your heart.*

*It's amazing what God will show you when you just believe!*

*Remember when your dad was lost so far in the things of this world?*

*Remember when your grandmother died?*

*Don't you remember when uncles on both sides of the family were physically and spiritually ill?*

*Remember when you thought your world had ended just because of life's trial?*

*Well, things turned around, didn't they...and there you are!*

*Sitting and waiting for the next obstacle so you can step on it.*

*You witness between light and darkness with the breaking of a new dawn—*

*How blessed you are to take another breath?*

*One thing I truly love about God's grace—is the simplicity.*

*He said He would never put more on us than what we could bear.*

*We as humans will never obtain the ability to grasp, in full, who God is.*

*His thoughts are deep and His ways are not our ways.*

*But God, still will perform miracles that only you can see.*

*I love how any specific trial can feel like the biggest one yet.*

*How will I ever make it through this; just take me now, Lord.*

*Prayer after prayer—what do I do, Lord—but I never waited for the answer.*

*Society's issue, even today, is that we don't know how to ask, wait, and then receive.*

*We want it hot and we want it now...spiritually speaking, it's the same thing.*

*We want what we want—where, how, and when we want it.*

*Never mind the fact that if God gave you a million dollars today, Your decisions would be far from pleasing and glorifying Him.*

*God's time may never seem like it will come—but He always seems to be on time!*

*Because of His faithfulness, we fail to realize—He's been carrying us through,*

*This whole time—through the storm, all along.*

*And Jesus was right there, aboard the ship—He never promised to take the storm.*

*But I know one thing He will do—He will keep us safe and warm.*

*We all must learn to walk one day.*

*He'll be with us every step of the way.*

*Stop trying to climb every mountain; God said tell it to move.*

*Don't look back, don't look to the left or right.*

*Just look up and you'll finally see,*

*That His Spirit is alive in you.*

## JUST WHEN

*Just when I thought it was my last breath...Ahhhhh!*

*Just when I thought I was at the end of the rope, I let go and realized my feet were*

*Planted.*

*Just when I thought there was no hope left for me, I looked up and got a burst of heaven!*

*Just when I thought I couldn't handle the hurt any longer, I fell to my knees and reached out a little further.*

*Just when I thought it was my last breath...Ahhhhh!*

*I exhale for the tears no one knows I cry.*

*I exhale for the sickness no one knows I carry.*

*I exhale for the wounds no one knows I cover.*

*I exhale for the life no one knows I almost lost.*

*I exhale for the battles no one knows I've fought.*

*I exhale for the healing no one knows I needed.*

*Just when I thought it was my last breath...Ahhhhh!*

*I exhaled for life.*

## *ANCHORED*

*In anger, I want to roar, show you I am a Lion. Tell you how if you step to me this ain't what you want, definitely not what you thought. Prove to you I don't need you to be afraid, just aware. Cut and slice with my words, tearing down your fraudulent confidence piece by piece—exposing the bare nothingness that is your reality. But instead, I bow in submission to the Holy Spirit's leading—knowing, in my meekness, the glory of God echoes throughout heaven's corridors…and the power inside that is the force that compels me…to choose life. I know it's easier to give in to the emotion. I know it's more pleasurable to appease the senses, but you don't mean that much to me. Giving up that energy to anyone strips me of my riches and my power. Without God, I'm not whole. I'm too poor to yield you my wealth. So, spew what you will, formulate notions to embellish your self-worth by discovering my flaws. Stand in the corner and whisper about my process. Don't invite me to the family gathering…it may hurt for a moment, but my eyes are on the prize. I look to heaven, knowing the author and finisher of my faith is a consuming fire, and He is for me. Come at me, but I warn you, I'm anointed!*

## WILL YOU PRESS

*"Fill my cup, Lord. High, lifted up, Lord. Come and quench this thirsting, in my soul. Bread from heaven, feed me, till I want no more. Fill my cup, fill it up, and make me whole."*

*Tears burn my face as they run down my cheeks. My heart races to keep up with the heavy breathing and the gasping for air. Remembering her touch, her sentiment.*

*Her sweet spirit brought light to any dark situation.*

*When she smiled, I knew then, that it was alright. Her discernment was incredible; it took you off guard because it was like she knew your whole story.*

*As I write, my fingers cramp, and my eyes are being veiled with tears.*

*She was God's light on Earth. She will be remembered from generation to generation.*

*Of the living water she indeed drank—her life completely defined God's love.*

*I think we'll never know the cost of the oil in her alabaster box.*

*For all her life, she poured her praise on the Master—I only hope to be the lady she was. I hear her telling me to walk in integrity and follow God's voice. Lord, speak to me.*

*I need to hear that whisper. My soul longs to be united with You— to be held in your arms, to lay in your bosom and be made over.*

*Shape me, mold me, and fix what is broken—I'm sending it back.*

*Through the shame that has crushed my face, pass the shadows of disgrace.*

*At last, I kneel before Your feet. I touched You. It was me, Lord.*

*I pressed, and I touched You. I need You to fill me—body, soul, and spirit.*

> *"...come and quench this thirsting in my soul. Bread from heaven, feed me, till I want no more. Fill my cup. Fill it up, and make me whole."*

## GRANDMA'S TRANSFORMATION

*When I think about transformation, I visualize change.*

*A decision one makes for things to be rearranged.*

*Being renewed is not always what it seems.*

*There was this image placed in my mind.*

*Yet when the time came, that image I did not find.*

*Instead, I experienced an abundance of peace.*

*This peace was full of love!*

*Love that promised never to leave me, hurt me, or confuse me.*

*It never leaves me wondering, nor with feelings of doubt.*

*It suffocated the very demons that tried to conquer my soul.*

*And made me realize that my assurance comes only from above.*

*This love has a name that is sweeter than the honey on a honeycomb,*

*Jesus is truly sweeter!*

*When my flesh was aching with uncontrollable pain,*

*I wanted to hide in the deepest hole and drown in the puddles of my tears.*

*Jesus told me it was ok—cry, my child—He said to me, cry.*

*Because I promise it will end with a smiling sigh.*

*And because her spirit lives on.*

*My soul has indescribable joy—how you might ask?*

*Because I know who my source is.*

*The source from which I come!*

*I'll never forget where He's brought me from.*

*I see my grandmother smiling at me.*

*She told me that she feels much better.*

*She says to me,*

*Remember His grace!*

*I do, cause now I see His face!*

*From glory to glory to glory!*

## WHEN I SAY I LOVE YOU

*When I say I love you, it's more than just a feeling.*

*I don't love you because I have this feeling—I have this feeling because I love you.*

*When I say I love you, it means I smile simply because you're smiling.*

*I'm content because you're ok.*

*When I say I love you, it's soul deep, not a midnight creep. I do what I do because it's the corresponding action. Love is kinetic energy. It moves, it does, and it shows.*

*When I say I love you, I compliment you and never degrade you; I support your goals and admire your ambition.*

*When I say I love you, I'm not saying this because it's what you want to hear.*

*Please, don't make I love you, only words in and out of your ear. Every pain, I want to know—and I'll listen to every tear as it falls. I want to know because your pain is my pain.*

*When I say I love you, I'm your help when you can't—your encourager, your friend, and comfort when you need it; the one to remind you, you are the workmanship of God.*

*I'll wipe your runny nose and feed you cheerios. I'll brush your hair to express my love and care. I want to know what you like, so it can become what I like.*

*I wanna know what you love, so it can become my love. I wanna see how much you love God, so we can grow to love Him more.*

*When I say I love you, it means sacrifice; it means dedication. It means I pray for you more than I pray for me. Love is the expressed image of commitment and passion.*

*If you can't eat, I'll eat for you. If you can't talk, I won't either. If you can't walk, I'll walk for you. If you lose your sight, I'll see you through. I'll describe each day with vibrant colors and bring you fresh flowers after the rain.*

*When I say I love you, I'm not just speaking words—I'm speaking life.*

*I'm saying for you I will and there is nothing that I won't do.*

*When I say I love you, I'm saying I do, til death do us part.*

## GOTTA GO

*So much of me wants to stay—see it reminds me of that song.*

*I don't really wanna go, I don't really wanna stay...*

*But you see the problem is we never got it together.*

*Did you even know what you did to me?*

*Is there any type of stimulation that shows you—you were my security and my nation?*

*I can't begin to explain how your eyes were a light that guided each step of my path.*

*How when your arms opened—there was I to fall within...explain something to me...*

*Why do us women give a man our all—the innermost part of our very being?*

*Then comes time when that sorry—low down—good for nothing...*

*Mmm, Lord—help my words—yall know what I wanna say.*

*This negro—yeah—he leaves y'all and acts as if he never believed.*

*I know it was you that said those things.*

*I know it was you with whom I shared my dreams.*

*Now at the blink of an eye you wanna tell me there's a significant other.*

*I don't understand this brother.*

*And you wonder why my sistahs are moving on and trying to stand strong.*

*Cause we sick—blue in the face and over being tried with all yo lies.*

*No—now, don't get me wrong,*

*Some of yall got sense and can tell when something so good comes into your grasp.*

*It's something you don't wanna let pass.*

*Nevertheless—your intentions may not have been to make me cry.*

*But please, tell me why—you did so much pimpin' and failed to realize?*

*That the very essence of my love—the sensual feel of my touch,*

*The passion behind my kiss—was just fading from view—which was you.*

*Now as I sit—giving serious and careful thought as to—why did I wait?*

*See, I should've been gone since that exact moment I saw you walking out her front door.*

*But you know what—it don't even matter no mo'.*

*Cause I've found a new light in life—I can't even begin to express from within.*

*Yet I'ma save that for later to let you know that I'm doing much better.*

*So as I walk the other way—no longer willing to stay,*

*I smile to myself—knowing—the next time you see me,*

*You'll wish you could be this free—I gotta go!*

## SATURATED IN THE BEAUTY OF LOVE

*Joy overfills me—happiness is all around me—peace abounds.*

*For I have life, and that more abundantly.*

*I can feel the vibrations in my spirit—moving up and down my spine,*

*Making me shiver.*

*Exquisitely beautiful!*

*Yes, God's love is certainly the beauty of them all!*

*He's holding me—He's comforting me—He's repairing me.*

*Healing my pain—providing my needs—wiping my tears completely dry.*

*But all I can ask is why?*

*Why do You love me like You do?*

*Why did You stay on that cross?*

*...just to save a wretch like me?*

*As I heard the voice—lo—calmness came over me.*

*Peace be still.*

*My sister, my friend.*

*I love you because My Father loves you.*

*And like My Father—love is Who I Am!*

*You are mine, I am yours, and we are His!*

*We are one!*

## STRAIGHT AND NARROW

*One day you're up, and the next you're not—you build up so much determination.*

*Telling yourself, I can do this—I've come too far to turn around now.*

*Tell me something—why it is at the weakest point in your life that hell and all its army come to hunt you down...*

*As a living witness—it's not all sunshine—it's not always eggs over easy.*

*Inevitably, the shadows come—oh, and they come when you least expect it.*

*Like a thief in the night, it prowls—waiting and waiting for the day it knows you'll fall.*

*Go away—what did I ever do to you, why me? Leave me alone!*

*These are the crazy thoughts that invade your mind—thoughts that tell you...*

*The devil is supposed to leave God's people alone—ha! Yeah, right.*

*Day by day, you tell yourself, this is becoming my new lifestyle— I'm getting the hang of it.*

*But where do the speed bumps originate? Why do they even appear?*

*Then you get all twisted up in this ball of confusion where you wrestle withing yourself.*

*You know—my mind's telling me no, but my body, my body...— don't even front.*

*Your body is telling you to do yo' thang—haven't I gotten passed this era?*

*Haven't I already conquered these demons?*

*How'd they get back in—on the inside—simply dying from deprivation.*

*You want so badly to just be caressed, touched, adored, held, and loved.*

*No, no—you gotta stay straight...and narrow.*

*How do I convince myself all over again? All the daylong, my mind is straying from purity.*

*Not purposely, but help!—this flesh is so persistent.*

*It's been a full year and now what...just start over...where do I attempt to start from?*

*Do I go right or do I go left? Go up, down, or side to side?*

*Step 1—yes, I'll obey, Step 2—application,*

*Step 3—learning to walk, Step 4—teach others,*

*How can I teach what I can't master myself?*

*Oh, and don't allow your mind to think of the pleasure because those thoughts alone...*

*Will make you do it again—even though you've fallen on your knees,*

*Time and time again.*

*You've got to be pure, inside and out.*

*And the patience of time is completely agonizing.*

*I want to crawl into something and never come out—as many times as you've thought this over in your mind—it still doesn't make sense...*

*Oh—now I remember...you told yourself this ain't no temptation for me—and then,*

*Oops—that's enough, stop—ok wait, no—it won't happen again— I promise.*

*Rising until the top is reached, and then it spills over and over and over until...*

*You lie there—expended—thoughtless, emotionless, speechless— and why?*

*Why you ask—it's the straight and narrow—yep!*

*Here we go again—grace, you got me?*

*Start back at one—straight...then narrow.*

# VOLUME 8

Everything was drastically changing. My perspective on life had received an extreme makeover. I didn't see the world through the same lens or with the same mind. I wanted authenticity so badly that it burned in my veins. Now, to only learn how to recognize it would be a bonus. My desires even shifted. I was no longer looking for completion or being whole from a man or any person, for that matter. God did that! I had so much to still learn, but every day was a different adventure of learning who I was becoming and who God knew all along that I'd be. I do remember being by myself more during that school year. I didn't want to hide anymore. I just wasn't interested or drawn by the same old things anymore—and make no mistake, change is never comfortable, and having to recalibrate your way of life amongst those who constantly remind you of you…is HARD! Hear me—the horizontal relationship with people makes this journey much more complicated than I know how to express. You ever prayed, "God, get your son," or "get your daughter?" Not like, get 'em, God, but like, Lord, do you see what your child just did? Can you please correct your child, please? I don't know, maybe it's just me. Maybe I'm at a loss for words on how to give a better description…LOL. However, God's grace is amazing and so much more! It is sufficient! Because of my blackout that summer, I wasn't going anywhere near alcohol. Yeah—blackout! I told you that summer was a dark, enlightening time—ironic, huh?! Dark and enlightening…all in one! I had a blackout—full blown lights out! I woke up with cold shower water bringing me back to reality. How did I go so low? It just had to be my birthday. Everyone throwing shots at you...who's keeping count—certainly, not me! They were for real, like, how many fingers are we holding up, and wouldn't take the water off of me until they believed my answers were lucid. Talk about worst moments. My two best friends were my angels that night. I didn't know it then, but these two would go on to become very crucial pieces in helping me define love, trust, loyalty, and friendship. Because of them, I am not quick to let just anyone have my heart. You can't un-know real friendship once you've had it; it taught me to guard my heart against a lot of heartache. Never think that because you give your true self that others will do the same in return. Don't assume the place you've given people in your heart and in your life is the same place they have given you in their life. So many factors go into that. They may not know how, they may not want to, or they may already believe what they're offering is the truest version of themselves. Of course, nothing is fool proof. I still had to learn, and I still am learning the depth, dynamic, and psychology of myself and other people. No two people are the same. Not all will be friends, but that shouldn't take away from the value they can add to your walk and experiences in life. I'm learning that a person cannot give you what they don't have. Too often, we're expecting people to love us, and they don't even love themselves or know themselves. How baby? How will they love us? They can't!...so back to that blackout. Needless to say, it scared me straight, but I still didn't want to admit it. I tried to drink again on another night and the taste made me completely sick. OK, Ok God! Cautiously and intentionally, this next semester's enjoyment came from being in my room listening to inspirational music, reading more about God, or just meditating. Yes, it may have started because I was shaking in my boots in terror from my "that only happens on TV" episode, but who cares how I got there. I was there baby…and have I got news for ya, I loved it! I learned so much about me, that it felt like I had met a new person, which I had. I learned so much about God's Word. I was learning to love it. That was some good stuff.

Some moments, I would reminisce about the "good ol' days," wondering if I missed them. They were all I had ever known. They were my fulfillment. They defined me—at least the only me I knew up to this point. They were my identity and who was I without them? I would replay different scenes in my mind; laughing about this and that, covering my mouth to contain the colorful memory. Soon, the incoming playback of the pain that came with those days would flood my brain receptors—a great reminder that it was nothing to go back to. For all the times I said, "God help," all the times I cried out from my emptiness—I was experiencing a sense of wholeness and I didn't want to lose it. It was like God was inducing my labor, metaphorically speaking. It was time to push forth the power that was in me all along. There were some wounds, some scars, some marred thinking, some memories, and some bad roots that needed to be flushed out, washed out, dug out—yanked out, flat out unlearned...so the me I was meant to be, could be birthed. The more I pushed, the more that void was filled with love and truth, and the more that was revealed.

Now, my head was at least turning in the right direction. I began focusing more on my studies. School became a priority instead of an option. I labeled my goals and took note of the steps I needed to take in order to reach them. Love and marriage were still in my view, but I wanted him to love God. I didn't want to compromise about that. I asked myself, if he doesn't love God and himself, how will he even begin to know how to love me—? What I liked most about my college days was the diversity. I've heard that children are like sponges and soak up any information you give them. Well, I was like a child again in that sense because I was soaking up so much. By now, my dad and I were the best of friends, and I was even soaking up knowledge from him. It was those days that I remembered him telling me about a quote on the day of my high school graduation from Shakespeare's *Hamlet*, "To thine own self be true." I carried that quote with me, and it became the words I've come to live by. To me, it meant knowing who I was without the influence of people's opinion altering that view. It was deciding to believe who God said I was, not people. Not only did I believe who God said I was, but I was also willing to be committed to her in every aspect. Don't ever let someone tell you who you should be or who you are until you have first checked in with your Creator. Yes, He will send people along the way to help mold, shape, and build you, but your identity should come only from who He has formed and called you to be.

Brand new, exposing, unhinged information was at my fingertips, and I couldn't see any logical reason to pass it up. I was even learning from the different guys that I would talk to. Some guys taught me how to respect myself solely based on how they would talk to or treat me and other girls. Their approach said a lot about them. Some guys were honest enough to admit their intent while others dangled charisma like Michael doing the moonwalk. Skills! They taught me what you don't know can and will hurt you. Naïve females taught me how to *get smart* quick. I mean, hello! I was naïve too! But I watched—I observed. I would sit in the barbershop for hours, laughing right along with them. I was one of them, or so it seemed. Harmless! They didn't have to talk much. Their interactions told the story. I also watched the naïve girls walk in, try to sit in the position I'd been granted—I'd see them fall and fail miserably. Then there were the *ghetto fabulous* girls. Ah naw, don't go pointing fingers at me (in my Bernie Mac voice)! Y'all know who these girls were. (*Ghetto fabulous:* a cultural mindset or label that females place on themselves, or that is environmentally or stereotypically given/titled to them) —I got a good laugh from them. They were pretty entertaining. They would go to the extreme just for a whistle from a guy walking by. The whole ordeal of games was all there was to life for them. Hours were spent to obtain this look. A look I still look at in confusion— oh my! Then, after their appetites were satisfied, they'd haul off to their dorm rooms to discuss every interaction from victims they had enticed. You had to be there! I had me some *ghetto fabulous* peeps. They were some of the coolest, sincerest people I had ever known. I will never forget the Homecoming when my cousin came to visit me. It meant EVERYTHING to me! She actually stayed in my dorm. Mind you, it wasn't allowed, but she blended right in. That visit was a whole vibe, y'all. I gave my cousin the best HBCU experience I could and then some. Baby…we partied, we danced, we sang, we ate, we mingled, and we laughed until it hurt—step shows, frat sets, fashion shows, you name it. All in one weekend! To this day, I'm thankful for the people I met, relationships I still have, and memories I created in college—good, bad, ugly, and indifferent because they are a part of me, and I have no shame, chile. It was all new exposure, though. I watched—listened— learned. It was life extended beyond the small scope 18 years in the Yak had provided. Pontiac was sheltered honey, but not in the sense that it was innocent or that it didn't have enough drama or trouble. It was small—too small—nowhere to escape or run to. I wanted to see life on the other side. I needed life from this perspective and that one too. Life is too big to only look like Pontiac. The experiences were all pieces to the artwork that would one day be me! Observation seasoned with the right information that simmers and presents revelation that leads to application is a great tool for adjusting a mindset, which is the start of changing a generation!

## THE WANTED NEED

*Sometimes we want something so badly that we try to make it a need.*

*This desire fills the desperate heart, and soon it drives you mad.*

*When you have something to say, at times, you can't find the words.*

*Then the confusion starts to jumble the mind, and your feelings seem so hard to find.*

*Why do we want these things so much that we can't see the reality?*

*To just let things come naturally right—else pain is shadowed by hostility, inevitably,*

*Waiting so long for yearned desires will rip you apart inside and out.*

*At last, the need has finally expired, but the feeling still—never truly a doubt.*

*If it were meant to have, time will reveal its hues.*

*Wants can wait without dispute, yet His supply for our needs is what I choose.*

## DIAMONDS OF LOVE

*Could a love be so strong as the current of the wind?*

*Could two come together as one?*

*Yes, this love I've found, cannot be measured,*

*For it covers the depths of my soul.*

*One might say, what do you know of love?*

*And I would answer, my heart knows.*

*For true love cannot be won by any fund.*

*Love is rare like a diamond,*

*And only for those that cherish it.*

*Will it last, as only precious jewels do?*

## THIS JOY I HAVE

*This joy I have,*

*The world didn't give me!*

*This joy I have,*

*I tell you, it set me free!*

*Turn my sorrows into day,*

*Now I know He's the only way!*

*Even though some times it gets rough,*

*I'm reminded that He's more than enough!*

*This joy I have,*

*The world didn't give me!*

*This joy I have,*

*I tell you, it set me free!*

*It will not be completely understood,*

*You see, I still cry.*

*But He dries my tears,*

*Just like He said He would.*

*At times, when I can't sleep at night,*

*I lift my head and look up.*

*There He is,*

*Guiding me with His light!*

*This joy I have,*

*The world didn't give me!*

*This joy I have,*

*I tell you, it set me free!*

*Chains no longer take hold,*

*For His grace is manifold.*

*Explanation is not my intent,*
*But rather, so you'll know what is meant,*
*When I say... This joy I have!*

## ENVIED

*I do not subscribe to, function according to, or live by the system created, by design, to alienate and identity strip by conversion of my person and spirit; including the conformity of my mind with the intention to control my behavior and thought patterns to fit into its overall plan wherewith I was not intended to partake in from its origin. I owe no man a definition or title of grouping for purposes of bias ranking and categorization. I am me!—perceive how you will. I am not feared, I am envied! Every convoluted, elaborate, but simple part of me. They fear the unknown, but I am not unknown. You already know the why—it's why your voyage was intended to transform my nature. What you don't know is how, and therein lies your hatred...deeply embedded; insidiously permeating your spiritual bloodline, infecting your DNA, causing generational decay. Those gallows—only reveal what man doesn't know. We speak of the foreshadows, the paid in full of what man owes, something about that name, hallowed—in me, was always greater than those, against me. He knows—my name, whereas what they meant for my downfall will not be how the plan goes. Need I remind you that He rose! Your footing is off-kilter, washed away as the river flows because your ground is a sinking hole. From time began until now, wrapped in divine, and it shows. He's sovereign—proceed cautiously with what you think you know— but by all means, continue to point your arrow and bow. In the end, you'll be the one in need. Desires emptied, for indeed, I am his seed. So my stance will remain—steady...I am me!—I am not feared, I am envied!*

## MY KIND OF WOMAN

*There she is—she's walking down the street,*

*With her head held high!*

*Yet still, more humble than you and I.*

*She goes about doing her thang.*

*Knowing her labor is not in vain.*

*There is no need to check her.*

*She comes from the One whom all blessings flow,*

*Just in case you didn't know!*

*She's that one we all wonder how, when, and where did she come from?*

*It never ceases to amaze me—how she walks and talks—cares and shares,*

*With even those, for her, aren't there.*

*Try not to stare.*

*Hmph!—She's my kind of woman!*

*Strong, black, and beautiful, a Nubian queen,*

*If you know what I mean!*

*From this very moment, I've known her for,*

*19 years—4 months—3 weeks—4 days—18 hours—23 minutes—and 6 seconds,*

*So it seems—but already I know.*

*She's my kind of woman!*

*I haven't began to tell you all that she's a child.*

*Of the One that hung, bled, and died—whose blood was shed on each side.*

*But because He rose on the 3<sup>rd</sup> day,*

*She knows—He made a way!*

*A way that her feet will not stumble.*

*For it is only the enemy that is in trouble.*

*She possesses beauty from within—beauty that is whole!*

*And sings sweet melodies to your soul!*

*I can only pray with hope that one day,*

*This same beauty can be found in her next of kin,*

*Again and again.*

*I have admired her since the beginning of my time.*

*And she's always on my mind—this lovely lady of mine!*

*She lights that flame that gives me the determination,*

*To do anything I claim.*

*By introducing me to my truest friend,*

*And showing me, I can do all things in Jesus name,*

*I say thanks because—She's my kind of woman!*

*Her style is truly original.*

*She can cook—and she's much smarter than your average gal.*

*The mother of seven—a loving and devoted wife,*

*And not to cause any strife—but um,*

*Yeah—I'm her baby.*

*And momma—you're my kind of woman!*

# VOLUME 9

Life has continued to teach me lessons. There is certainly a consequence to every action. I now live by a different creed. I don't blame others for the outcome of my life or for the consequences of my choices. I determine which direction I will travel, which is the Master's way. Though I had accepted Christ at an early age, this was an encounter like none other. God introduced me to His Spirit. I got to know Him. He's the sweetest, most genuine, and strongest force I know. I came to love Him, and now I have the revelation of who He is and what He does and did for me. He was there the *whole* time. He is Sovereign, He just is; that settled inside my entire being. And not all at once, but with time, it is starting to all make sense. Every step I had taken was all in preparation, and still is, of where He is—and has always been leading me. Through these poems, God gave me a way of escape—a voice to speak, a way to cope through the struggles, and a word to be heard…a prayer to be whispered. Life happened to me. Life happens to us all. Some scenes in your story may be much worse than mine, I'm sure. Childhood and its effects are inevitable, but doing the work—digging up the toxic roots to be a healthy adult to yourself first and then to others is a choice. I make that choice every day that God allows His grace to enable me— not to specialize in other people's opinion of me, but rather to fall in love with the best version of myself and continue to allow her to be set free—daily. Love has a corresponding action, and it doesn't mistreat or misuse. I will remember my journey and say

Love was waiting for me. Love was protecting me. Love was disciplining me. Love was teaching me. Love was covering me. Childhood gave me some ugly experiences, false definitions, and scars that made me believe love hurts. God is love, and love doesn't hurt. People hurt! Abuse, in all its forms, hurts! Rejection hurts! Being lied to hurts! Abandonment hurts! Disloyalty hurts! Betrayal hurts! Love is relentless and never gave up on me—never let me down. Love chose me and chooses me every day. Love came after me. I was pursued. There is a story behind every tear—a seed to every field's harvest. Through my experiences, I know that my parents, siblings, etc., and environment had a huge impact on who I was—and it wasn't all bad. However, I choose who and what has the impact on who I am. And today, I can gladly and thankfully say, I wouldn't change the outcome one bit. I love me, I love my parents—I honor them; I love my beautiful siblings. I'm thankful for them being there for me, helping me, protecting me, and loving me... and most importantly, Yahweh loves all of me and I love Him! Hey guys, He loves all of you too! I sum that up by saying—I am so loved— you are so loved—arrested and charged—loved by an everlasting, ever-loving, ever-giving love! Don't ever think you've drifted so far away or done something so bad that God's love can't reach you. There is nothing big enough or strong enough to keep God from getting to you. Do the work—it's worth it. It takes discipline; it takes effort. It takes talking it out, writing it out, screaming it out. It takes prayer and feeding your soul and energy with the right stuff. Yeah, you'll mess up at times, I still do—but getting up and deciding not to give up on yourself is a superpower. God is pursuing you…pursue Him back and watch things turn around for you. The best thing about God's love—it's the same, yesterday, today, and forever! Love didn't change on me, but instead, Love changed me!!!

## AN UNDESERVED LOVE

*Thank You, Father, for this time of consecration,*

*For peace in my soul and clarity in my spirit.*

*Thank You, Father, for Your presence.*

*Thank You, Father, for Your voice that comes in a still whisper.*

*Thank You, for Your sweet touch.*

*Thank You, for Your love,*

*A love I shall never understand.*

*Thank You, for choosing me.*

*I'll never fully grasp the magnitude of Your love.*

*Thank You, for not leaving me in my mess.*

*I'll never understand so great a love.*

*I'll never know how much it cost.*

*I'll never understand why—my soul, You spared?*

*What is man that You are mindful of him?*

*I'll never understand.*

*But I'm so grateful and I embrace this love.*

*I embrace it with all I am,*

*With everything I have,*

*And in all that I do.*

*I embrace an undeserved love.*

## THE BEST MAN

*Hey ladies, guess what?! I know a man that exceeds your best dreams!*

*Everything you could possibly think of, He is!*

*I know you think I'm fantasizing, but truth is—*

*I was maximizing everything that I should've been minimizing.*

*And now I'm realizing that He's all the man I need!*

*I don't have to fake it cause He knows me better than I know myself.*

*He knows how to hold me when I need it most.*

*Wipes each tear as it falls down my face.*

*A listening ear, true and sincere.*

*This man, I tell you—is all the man I need!*

*When I need a helping hand—He's my man.*

*If I'm falling off track—He's got my back.*

*Let's me know that I also have a friend in Him.*

*Keeps me on the right path—not hesitating to tell me when I'm wrong.*

*While all along, assuring me—by His side is where I belong.*

*No private love here—He openly showers me!*

*Tender touches, sweet embraces,*

*I know now—He's all the man I need!*

*Did I mention that He spends time with me?*

*Intimate time—time where I learn of Him.*

*Learning how His love is patient and kind, selfless and gentle, forgiving and enduring*

*Learning how His love never fails.*

*Whenever I need Him…He's immediately near—erasing all fear!*

*He's my comfort, He's my strength…a breath of fresh air!*

*He's my friend, He's my love!*

*The man named Jesus—is all that I needed most!*

## MY FIRE

*This fire in me is burning!*

*It burns the walls of my bones!*

*It is ripping apart the structure of my body's frame!*

*People don't always understand this flame.*

*But they do sense the presence!*

*This fire won't let me give up.*

*Constantly pushing me to the top!*

*When others tell me what I can't do,*

*Y'all know haters hate,*

*Don't be surprised—that's what they do,*

*That's when my fire begins to blossom!*

*It grows deeper into the borrows of my inner man.*

*Uplifts my eyes above and tells me to go forward,*

*Do not look back.*

*It encompasses my faith and prepares me for the battle's attack.*

*I can do this—my race is not for man!*

*I'm running with my savior,*

*My best friend, my comforter,*

*My strength, my Father—He's my everything!*

*He is my fire!*

*It is Him who lives in me!*

*It is Him that gives me authority and power!*

*I have boldness and I have dominion!*

*And one thing my enemy can never face,*

*Is the word of truth!*

*This is—the path I trace … This is—whom I serve.*

*He is the only one that can give me sufficient grace.*

*And because He ignites this fire in me,*

*I cannot, will not—and I shall not fall!*

# ABOUT THE AUTHOR

Erinn Imari is a Pontiac, Michigan native and currently resides in Nashville, TN. She has been writing since age 9 and her dad was behind the inspiration for her to allow others to hear what he called "a gift." That took a while to muster the courage. Since then, Erinn has done open mic at several poetry lounges, weddings, schools, churches, and various events. She has always emphasized loving her freedom of expression with poetry and that it's a feeling you can't hide. Erinn is the mother of 2 beautiful daughters, Amariah and Eden, and becoming their mother propelled her, even further, into being the best version of herself. Children see right through you! Life is all about the thorns and the rose. It's not ever only easy, but trouble is also not in charge, nor does it last always.

In her free time, Erinn enjoys reading, dancing, being silly with her daughters, playing volleyball, and singing; mostly, she loves to enjoy loved ones and to just live in those moments as her authentic self...good and bad, growing and thriving. Erinn is passionate about encouraging others and telling them what God has said about them while helping them acknowledge and become who He says they are. Identity! So often we believe the lie; so, sharing God's truth about us to other individuals brings her joy. Erinn has a very quirky and serious, but silly personality, and most times, people's first impressions are way off! God is her lover, and she's sold out to Him with all her heart and soul! She's very much aware of His love for and towards her. Because of that love, she is brave enough to share what He has brought her through and done for her.

Erinn now declares, "I am enough!" and it took a very long time to believe and know that for herself. God has caused Erinn to become free! Her hope and desire is that others will receive that same freedom through trusting God in the process as well as the process itself. She prays others receive His truth about who we are and allow Him to walk us into the version of ourselves that only He knows! Because He is, after all, the Creator!

www.ingramcontent.com/pod-product-compliance
Lightning Source LLC
Chambersburg PA
CBHW060520130626
46553CB00002B/583